GOD'S PANACEA

Through the archway of the 12 steps to Freedom

By

Roxanna Bennett Carrothers

Dedicated to the lost boys

Frankie

Dylan

Kolby

John

And a girl

Zoe

God's Panacea © 2018 by Roxanna Bennett Carrothers

Printed in USA

PREFACE

A panacea is a solution for all difficulties, the universal cure for all problems. It is someone or something that makes everything about a situation better.

The age old wisdom of our predecessors, the saints, philosophers, seers, poets and prophets is that God is that panacea. God as Father, God as Trinity, God as Nature or God as Good Orderly Direction. No doubt they all had individual and unique experiences that led them to their conclusions. In many cases we are able to find the personal experiences in their writings. Individual experiences that led them to a conclusion that God was the ultimate panacea to humanity's problems.

Had the title been available, I would have called this book *God Has No Grandchildren. As* that has been the thinking many before me had found to be true in their lives. The conclusion being: you can't give your understanding of God to someone else and have it serve them in their life. You can't catch God like you can catch the measles. God is an experience as individual as every star, as every snowflake and as every living individual.

Life prompts me to discover and/or experience the God that is personal to me but I can't use yours. Your belief and example may stir a yearning in me to find my own, but yours will not be sufficient, as my journey is not yours.

It has been proven that we each are as different as the snowflakes that fall on earth. Based on that finding, we can assume that we each have our own unique purpose, our own path and our own reason for being. Therefore, the panacea we must find is also as different from each other as night is from day.

The same can be said of all the leaders, prophets and seers of the Old and New Testament. All are so very different and all with their own purpose, each supplied with the skills necessary to complete the plan destiny held for them.

How can God fill the need of the lives of so many, unless He is large enough to be the panacea to all life? Of course, if He is the creator of life and nature, then He could be large enough to be everything to all. As has been said of Him, God explains life - God sustains life - God completes life. Perhaps for the Christian it can explain how He took twelve men, as different from each other as possible and had all but one come away in perfect unison of the same purpose each in their own individual way. The one man also had a purpose but when he didn't fulfill it, he chose death.

This rings true with the quote of C.S. Lewis, "To walk out of God's will is to walk into nowhere."

To the Jewish community I offer this thought, every one of God's prophets, all different, all with a specific purpose and all fulfilled His purpose, even when humans tried to divert His purpose.

Carl Jung, noted psychiatrist, concluded with his work on himself and his patients that life has a spiritual purpose beyond material goals. Our main task, he believed, is to discover and to fulfill our deep innate potential. Based on his study of Christianity, Hinduism, Buddhism, Gnosticism, Taoism, and other traditions, Jung believed this journey of transformation, which he called individuation, is the mystical heart of all religions. **It is a journey to meet the self and at the same time the Divine.**

The concept, to meet the self, and at the same time the Divine, implies action. Meet is a verb that means, in this instance, to come into the presence or into the company of. Much like the verbs seek and knock. Seek and you will find, knock and it will be open.

God is universally accepted as synonymous with love. Not just love in the human sense, but love in the broadest sense. Unconditional, all inclusive, all fulfilling, all satisfying, answering all, being all and filling a yearning that many are unaware of even knowing they are in want of. In other words, He completes life.

Examination of my own life has led to finding God as the explanation for life. As I go deeper into this belief, I find He completes my life and brings peace into all areas of my life. I have found that I am made for eternity and this life is meant to build on the firm foundation of faith. This is one phase of my life and it is important how I make preparation for the next stage. For my belief is that there are no endings, only new beginnings. My first was to come into the world with no knowledge of the one I left. My second journey is to go back to the origin of my being with knowledge of where I am going.

To bring a formula that can be used into the present day, where all who may be seeking a spiritual solution to their life, is what I hope this book can be for the seeker. Also, I hope it can bring renewed energy for those that life has made weary and they seek companionship and affirmation on their journey.

Like the original book, Alcoholics Anonymous, I am incorporating individual stories of people who have used these 12 steps in their lives. Each has experienced a change sufficient to undergo a spiritual upheaval that impacted their lives. They have moved to a place of peace and serenity, formerly unknown to them.

No smoke and mirrors. No expensive therapy. No gimmicks. The only requirement is to add these principles to your life, one day at a time, to the best of your ability.

Unlike the original Big Book, the stories here will take the experiences of people from all different twelve step programs. Hopefully, you can find your story and use the same solution to find peace.

In this day and age, an opioid addiction epidemic is sweeping the world. It is killing hundreds of thousands of our youngest and most promising children. They are seeking a solution to living and are actually victims of a system that offers no help, only more drugs. The well-intentioned keep paving the road to death and to hell because of their inability to understand and treat addiction.

The drug companies prosper either in their addictive drugs bought on the street, or their so called treatment drugs used as a cure by almost all treatment facilities and detox centers. In essence, the system is pouring water on drowning people's heads.

I am suggesting a return to a program of action that is still viable and ignored by many who only breezed through the initial process and declared that it didn't work. They seem to be believed more than the millions who have had a changed life because of this program. The twelve steps followed in a person's life, in their entirety to the best of someone's ability on a daily basis guarantees sobriety, sanity and an individual spiritual solution to the thirst, self-hate, anger and depression found in the addict. It gives the addict a 24 hour reprieve from death and destruction that they so earnestly seek in their addiction.

Because it is free, it is ridiculed as old and ineffective. No one pays attention to the thousands who have spent millions of dollars on other programs, only to find their solution in this simple program of love, attraction and action.

As I see what is happening all around I think of something my Father said many years ago. He was asked, "If they found a cure or a pill that cured alcoholism would he take it?"

He replied, "I wouldn't take it or anything to change what I have been given today. I have peace, self-respect, a loving God, fellowship, love and purpose. How will they put that in a pill?"

Pax Vobiscum (Peace be with you)

Roxanna Bennett Carrothers

CHAPTER 1

A NEW LIGHT HAS ENTERED THE DARK WORLD OF HUMANITY

A book called Alcoholics Anonymous was brought into the world in 1939. It featured a design for living that included 12 steps that promised to bring a spiritual solution into your life, as well as an awakening experience by step 12. It was a very tall order and at the time, it was a book exclusively for alcoholics and addicts.

Shortly after the book release, a Jesuit priest by the name of Father Dowling, who was not an alcoholic or an addict, sought out the author of these 12 steps, Bill Wilson, because he felt that what Bill Wilson had done in 12 steps had taken his religion many years to teach. Father Dowling also believed that these 12 steps could help any person with any defect, problem or difficulty regardless if they were alcoholic or not.

There are now more than 40 separate groups that use these same 12 steps, with a simple modification to step 1. I believe Father Dowling was correct.

I have firsthand experience with Alcoholics Anonymous and Al-Anon. I hope to share the idea of how your life can be fulfilling, as a result of applying these steps, once day at a time. The steps were designed to take you towards mental, emotional and spiritual freedom.

My Father passed away just shy of 56 years in the highly spiritual program of Alcoholics Anonymous (hereafter referred to as AA) He joined AA in 1948,nine years after the introduction of the book Alcoholics Anonymous, which was to change the course of history.

To clear up any confusion there are two different AA's when referring to Alcoholics Anonymous. The first is the meeting that transpired in 1935 (the birth date of AA) between Dr. Bob Smith and Bill Wilson. That grew into the program of action, AA meetings, that still thrive today. The second reference is the book Alcoholics Anonymous (the Big Book} first published in 1939, the handbook used by the members in AA, the program.

Here I would beg of you, if alcoholism and/or drug addiction is not your problem, when I use the word, "alcohol", please substitute the defect from which you are seeking freedom. The original 12 step program is being used for smoking, overeating, sexual permissiveness, emotions, gambling, work, etc. etc.

Saint Paul said, "All have sinned and all are guilty"', so I assume this includes all who are reading this book.

In order to give a foundation for the twelve steps, a brief history of AA would be beneficial for any who are seeking to integrate these steps into their lives. It is most helpful to see how the program was most assuredly inspired by a Power much greater than any one of the individuals used to bring this salvation into fruition.

A man of wealth and position was afflicted with alcoholism. Unable to stop drinking through every means available early the 1930's, he made the trip by boat to meet with Dr. Carl Jung, in Zurich. His name was Roland Hazard. He stayed there for almost one year under the care of Dr. Jung. He was on his way back home feeling cured of alcoholism but before he reached the shores of home he was drunk again. He returned to Dr. Jung, who pronounced he had no cure for him. If this doctor had offered his visitor a pill or any other therapy, there certainly would not be a 12 step program today.

Roland asked Dr. Jung "is there nothing left for me?"

To which Dr. Jung responded, "Yes, there is. Exceptions to cases such as yours have been occurring since early times. Here and there, once in a while, alcoholics have had what are called vital spiritual experiences." He went on to describe a spiritual experience "To me these experiences are phenomena. They appear to be in the nature of huge emotional displacements and rearrangements. Ideas, emotions, and attitudes which were once the guiding forces of the lives of these men are suddenly cast to one side, and a completely new set of conceptions and motives begin to dominate them" (pages 26/27 in the book Alcoholics Anonymous, hereafter referred to as the Big Book). The humble doctor admitted his failure in bringing about this psychic change and dashed this man's hope that his past strong religious convictions alone could bring on a "vital spiritual experience".

On returning home, he joined the Oxford Group, a group of men and women practicing first century Christianity, at that time led by Dr. Samuel Shoemaker. The tenets of the Oxford Group were 1. Admit hopelessness 2. Get honest with self 3. Get honest with another 4. Make amends 5. Help others without demand 6. Pray to God as you understand Him.

Roland would help rescue his friend, Ebby Thatcher, from a jail sentence and introduce him to the Oxford Group. Ebby Thatcher, in return, is the man who would carry the message of the Oxford Group to his friend Bill Wilson who had been given a death sentence if he continued drinking. One of the tenets of the Oxford Group was the need to share their experience of redemption with another, carrying the message.

The Doctor, Dr. Silkworth, who treated Bill in Towns hospital, was convinced through his work with alcoholics that they suffered from a physical allergy to alcohol. The allergy, along with a mental obsession to continue once the allergen was introduced into the bodies of those with this disease, seemed to doom them to early deaths or insanity. This allergy also was accompanied by a peculiar mental twist. Although these men he treated appeared normal in every other respect, when it came to alcohol they were unable to leave it alone, even when it meant the loss of family, homes, jobs etc.

Dr. Silkworth was the first medical professional to call alcoholism a disease.

The history is relevant because we now have the three vital concepts that are going to bring healing to people that before had to die of the disease. Or once in a while, every now and then would have a spiritual experience that could alter their lives. The three separate ideas that consolidated in the mind of Bill Wilson, came from three distinct non-alcoholic sources. These would result in the 12 steps that would launch a new cure into the world for all the ills of mankind.

The three basic elements of the AA program are A) the problem; which came from Dr. Silkworth, the allergy and the peculiar mental twist. B) The program of action, based on the main principles of the Oxford Group, which Roland brought to Ebby who in turn shared with Bill. Originally Bill used six steps based on the teaching of the Oxford Group. The Oxford Group was founded by a Lutheran minister who wanted to recreate first century Christianity. C) The solution, credited to Dr. Carl Jung, a noted psychiatrist in Switzerland. The solution had to be a spiritual solution as the good doctor explained he had no other cure to offer.

From these three sources came the program Alcoholics Anonymous. This is the foundation from which the many other programs based on AA have stemmed. To comprehend these set of circumstances coming into being from so many places and all centering around one alcoholic is nothing short of a miracle.

The history is available in books, online and many web sources. The success of just this one program is staggering.

As of January 1, 2017 in the United States there were more than 61,258 groups with 1,276,165 members. In Canada there were 5,078 groups with 86,237 members. In correctional facilities there were 1,413 groups with 34,903 attendees. Outside Canada and the U.S. there were 50,555 groups with 705,850 registered members. This are registered groups and members. Many small groups and also some very large ones are not included in this tally as they do not report to the General Service Office.

The numbers speak for themselves along with the offshoot programs using the same formula.

I cannot fail to mention Dr. Bob Smith, the co-founder along with Bill Wilson of AA. He and Bill were as different as night and day except they both suffered with alcoholism. Their personalities were both needed to bring this program to the public and into practice and fruition. The one without the other would have surely left the world without the light and solution to many age old problems.

Chapter 2

FELLOWSHIP

Friendship is born at that moment when one person says to another:
What! You too?
I thought I was the only one.
C.S. Lewis

As Bill Wilson explained on page 17 of the Big Book, we are people who normally would not mix. But there exists among us a fellowship, friendliness, and an understanding which is indescribably wonderful. The feeling of having shared in a common peril is one element in the powerful cement which binds us. But that in itself would never have held us together as we are now joined.

The tremendous fact for every one of us is that we have discovered a common solution. We have a way out on which we can absolutely agree, and upon which we can join in brotherly and harmonious action.

The basis of all 12 step programs is the identity with another person who is suffering from the same peril. That will bring them together, and the only thing that will hold them together is working the same solution, each on a journey uniquely their own, with the same directions. Each is traveling at a different pace and each with a different understanding of the directions. All are lead into a new freedom and new understanding of their own life journey.

Bill Wilson set about in the AA program to build an actual archway where the person applying these principles (steps) in their lives would be able to walk through this archway into freedom. This would be the same formula that anyone in a 12 step program would experience as they apply these principles to their life.

Before describing the arch let me present the 12 steps of the AA program as outlined in the Big Book.

1. We admitted we were powerless over _____, that our lives had become unmanageable. (In the case of AA this would be alcohol)

2. Came to believe that a Power greater than ourselves could restore us to sanity.

3. Made a decision to turn our will and lives over to the care of God as **we understood Him.**

4. Made a searching and fearless moral inventory of ourselves.

5. Admitted to God, to ourselves, and to another human being the exact nature of our wrongs.

6. Were entirely ready to have God remove all these defects of character.

7. Humbly asked Him to remove our shortcomings.

8. Made a list of all persons we had harmed, and became willing to make amends to them all.

9. Made direct amends to such people except to do so would injure them or others.

10. Continued to take personal inventory and when we were wrong promptly admitted it.

11. Sought through prayer and meditation to improve our conscious contact with God **as we understood Him,** praying only for

knowledge of His will for us and the power to carry that out.

12. Having had a spiritual awakening as the result of these steps, we tried to carry this message to _____, and to practice these principles in all our affairs. (In the case of AA this would be alcoholics)

13. Having concluded the 12 steps there are three pertinent ideas:

    (a)   That we were _____ and could not manage our own lives. (In this case alcoholic)

    (b)   That probably no human power could have relieved our _____. (In this case alcoholism)

    (c)   That God could and would if He were sought.

Let's proceed to the triumphant arch with Bill Wilson's description.

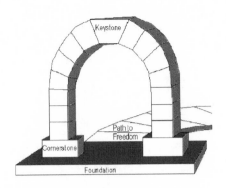

The Bedrock: Our admissions of personal powerlessness finally turned out to be the firm bedrock upon which a happy and purposeful life may be built.

The Foundation: I saw that growth could start from being willing to believe in a Power greater then myself.

The Cement: The feeling we have shared in a common peril is one element in the cement that binds us. The other is we have found a common solution. (The steps)

The Cornerstone: Do I now believe or am I willing to believe that there is a Power greater than myself? If a man can answer yes it has been proven that upon this simple cornerstone a wonderfully effective spiritual structure can be built.

The Keystone: First we had to quit playing God. It didn't work. Next we decided that God was to be our Director. He is the Father, and we are His children. This concept was the keystone of the new and triumphant arch through which we passed to freedom.

The Foundation Stone: Helping others is the foundation stone of your recovery. You have to act the Good Samaritan every day, if need be.

The Path to Freedom: Looking again at the first five steps we ask if we have omitted anything, for we are building an arch through which we shall walk a free man at last. Is our work solid so far? Are the stones properly in place? Have we skimped on the cement put into the foundation? Have we tried to make mortar without sand?

The word fellowship is also an interesting choice for any group of likeminded people. Fellowship according to the dictionary is "a group of equals." So no one in a fellowship is above the other regardless of the time anyone has been practicing the steps. This gives another aspect of the humility that one must acquire for the practice of these steps and any 12 step program in one's life. There is no higher authority than one's own concept of a Higher Power that is individual to them.

Hence a vital spiritual experience, where one casts aside old ideas, and attitudes and are changed from what they were into more of what they wished to become.

The success of applying this formula to any and all problems that affect one's life, livelihood and family is well proven as perhaps the best and only formula that works.

Many to most treatment facilities where people go to detox add a 12 step program as a requirement of being a resident there. They bring in people from 12 step programs to work with clients in rehabs and detox, and have them offer the clients the 12 step way of life.

Since 1939 it has proven to be one of the most successful programs for abstinence and also the most inexpensive.

If you have a dollar, you can put it in the basket when they pass it or you can stay if you have no money. There are no dues or fees.

All 12 step programs are formed and survive on the identification or belonging to a group of people who have the same malady or defect that is ruining your life. No one truly understands what a person is experiencing or living unless they have lived the same problem.

We can have all the empathy in the world for someone suffering from something we have not experienced but we cannot really offer any hope or help without firsthand knowledge of their experience.

I have friends with MS and I have compassion for them but can no more identify with the process of the disease and the real impact on them physically.

I experienced the loss of a child and until I did I thought I could relate and offer sympathy to those who did. When the reality of that experience happened to me I realized how feeble my understanding had been.

A fellowship of equals is the most therapeutic experience one can have because you speak the same language. The language that says, "me too". It is a bond of understanding one cannot get from a book. To experience that bond and a solution to the problem unites them in a way that is uniquely wonderful.

Chapter 3

FLOYD

We are changed from character to character, from tenderness to tenderness.
Henry Drummond

He was born an identical twin in 1915, Floyd and Lloyd. He was one of eight children. His father died when he was eight, six years before the actual start of the great depression. This would shape his resentment of a God that would take his Dad away, when he was so loved and needed. He refused to cry.

Times were hard for all families let alone such a large family with no Father. Families were separated as the need to feed the youngest fell as a burden on the older children. Many times children were taken in by a family that had fewer children and the ability to feed an extra mouth. They didn't get to experience their youth as they were burdened with the overwhelming responsibility to help one another survive under extremely difficult circumstances.

In 1933 the CCC camps of Michigan formed. It provided an opportunity for young men to have a job and earn some money. In the mid 1930's Floyd and his twin Lloyd enrolled in the program and agreed to send $22 of their $30 dollar monthly wages home to family.

Floyd often talked of the love he had for the moonshiner's daughter in those northern woods of Michigan in the early 30's. Years later he would mention her and say, "And I love her daddy still." Those days, in the CCC camp, were spent in hard labor during the week and weekends drinking with new found friends who were all young and experiencing life away from home. Being an identical twin added some extra benefits such as doing double row call duty at bedtime for one another if one of them happened to not be back at the appropriate time.

So drinking was a part of his early days and continued when he left the CCC camp and began married life.

Floyd was married at 22 and his children came quickly. He worked with a friend painting and manual labor to earn money. Many times with money in hand he found his way to a bar and didn't come home until his money was gone.

In 1941 when the famous Jack Alexander article from the Saturday Evening Post hit the streets, Floyd's mother rushed to give her 26 year old son the article. She thought the story on Alcoholics Anonymous could possibly hold a cure him. But she found him in jail singing mademoiselle songs. He had two children and lost one by this time. And his mother was still trying to help him in any way she could.

The information that is known for sure is he had three children and lost one child at her birth. He loved women and drinking and by the time he was 32 he lost his very modest home and wife and family because he found himself unable to give up the alcohol for anyone or anything. His wife went home with her three children and moved in with her Mother. She found a job as a barmaid in an American Legion club. She raised their three children virtually alone. The person he had become was a man held in low esteem by his community, family and friends.

He found AA in the small town of Owosso, Michigan, sometime in early 1946, and attempted to stay sober to win back his wife and family but that wasn't to be. After a brief set back he made it back to AA later that year and he never drank again. He died a sober man at 86.

Perhaps what transpired in his life through sobriety is the real story. He never left that small town where he had become so ill thought of because of his life. What he became was a man well respected and loved. He remarried. He ran for mayor and lost by a narrow margin. He sold insurance for a living and he set about applying the principle of helping others as a way of life. The man who he had been was gone and he had been changed into the man he was created to be. The lives he changed and saved in the town became well known. He was loved and admired for the sacrifices of time he gave to every person he met who had a need. Whether it was the president of a company or the man coming from the river bank needing 50 cents, they were all treated with the same love and respect.

The men who knew him in the early days referred to him as Bennie. They were witness to the change and transformation that took place in him through the years. Many came to him because they believed if he could change perhaps they could too.

20

The power of attraction.

The change had to be real because alcoholics can spot a phony a mile away. Let alone that for the next 56 years of his life that change that had occurred remained and grew in love and service.

This is the man I called Dad.

Chapter 4

DAD

All I have seen teaches me to trust the Creator
for all I have not seen.
Ralph Waldo Emerson

The idea of the results of a life lived in a 12 step program is exemplified by my Father. I watched him through the years as he grew and changed into the kind of loving man he was meant to be. It radiated from him and he attracted all who wished to be embraced in that love. He often used these same words to describe his own sponsor (the person who takes someone through the 12 steps)

This man told my Dad, "if you stick around you will find more love here, than in any other organization in the world." He said, "And that includes the Masons." As my Dad explained, he had no idea what a Mason was, but this man was a power of attraction to my Dad. Before my Father died he became a 32nd degree Mason.

Here are two men, my Father and his sponsor, changed and transformed into examples of love and service by the same 12 step program. Both men are examples of lives changed and transformed into the most useful kind of existence by the Divine grace of the God of their understanding.

These are only two men, and I have been privileged to know so many more like them. These are men and women who normally wouldn't mix. But they have been rescued from seemingly hopeless lives and they are joined in brotherly love by sharing a common solution.

Once these people find an answer to their living problem and experience a loving Higher Power, they become pillars of society. Once so lost and having been found, they never forget where they have been. They are the first ones there when love, compassion and understanding are needed. They don't look down on anyone because they understand, having been there themselves.

I grew up a part of this fellowship of love and giving. AA in the nineteen fifties and sixties was a wonderful place to be. The AA and Al-anon (family and friends of the alcoholic) groups would have wonderful get-togethers with food, games, and good conversation. I learned what a great time can be had without alcohol being added to the party. In comparison to parties with alcohol, I have come to prefer the ones without.

I also learned AA was not a cult or weird religion. No one ever forced religion or God on me. Everyone had their own personal belief and their own personal expression of that belief. It didn't matter what that religion was. Catholic, Episcopalian, Lutheran, Jewish, etc... I am sure they were all represented but it wasn't a focus or requirement.

It reminded me of the words of St. Francis, "Preach the gospel always and if necessary use words."

The actions of these people were the 12 steps of AA and the practice of them in their lives.

They loved each other and were there night and day for one another. They celebrated happy times and supported each other through sad times. They were a fellowship in every sense of the word.

And as for my Father, he was a light to all he met. He was a hugger and this included the women and the men. He called it an "embracio" (hug) although he wasn't Italian. He would lift you off your feet as he wrapped his arms around you. He loved to sing and he walked around town whistling and greeting everyone he met. He drew no distinction, if they were breathing he greeted them with a smile.

Of all the people I met in the program I believe he enjoyed his sobriety perhaps the most. He sponsored so many men that there was always someone in our apartment. They worked on steps, listened to records of the early AA members, played cribbage or just talked. He always had time to listen and to share his experience with the newcomers. He loved to golf and golfing always included being with his fellows in the program.

His golf game and his cribbage were things of legends. At golf he would use a tee all the way to the green unless he was caught. He would find his opponents ball and accidently step on it, driving his opponent's ball deep into the ground, as he made his way to his ball. This was a usual happening and no one believed it was an accident. He could work magic with his score so he usually came out a few shots short of what had been counted.

He had heard about a cure a doctor was working on with alcoholics that involved taking niacin. Although it never proved to be a cure one of the effects of high dosages of niacin is feeling as though you are on fire. He found that if he gave his golf opponents a few mgs of niacin before the game, all because he was concerned for their health, they ended up being very uncomfortable by the third hole. This usually affected their game and he coolly played on.

His cribbage game was also one of infamy. He was known to move pegs so swiftly that they would end up a street ahead of the place they should be.

His motto was, if there is no trickery, he won't play. And miracles of miracles he never was in need of cribbage players or golfers as everyone truly loved being with him. I think in retrospect he did a lot for the people who have to win or they don't enjoy the game. To Dad, even if he didn't win he was going to enjoy it.

The stories of him and the love and fellowship he shared and the joy of helping others are still remembered by so many who knew him.

He experienced AA in the early years and met the men who pioneered the program. He ran men from mid-Michigan to the hospital in Ohio where Dr. Bob and Sister Ignatia were caring for so many. It was one of the few places that would take the drunks in for help.

What I remember most is the love these men had for one another. It was the true result of people living the steps in their everyday lives. It was remarkable to see.

When I was in high school, we lived on Main Street, in a small town. My Father had his car parked on the street. He hadn't moved it to the parking lot for the night yet. We were finishing dinner and we heard a loud crash on the street in front of our apartment. Looking out the window we saw a car had just smashed my Dad's car and was hobbling away down the street although they were pretty damaged also from the wreck. Living a block from the police station they were immediately at the scene. By the time we went downstairs the police were hauling the driver of the car into their police car. My Dad's car was totaled.

What my Dad did next says everything about him and this way of life. He went to the jail which was a block away in the police station and spoke with the man. His name was Ron. Ron had been celebrating his wife having a baby and was very drunk. My Dad talked to him about AA that night. He never pressed charges. He never expressed anger, only compassion for Ron. Ron joined AA and never drank again until his death. My Dad became his sponsor.

Dad had wanted one of his pigeons (as a sponsee used to be called) to read a book that had a profound impact on his life. He shared this book with everyone he met. It was *The Greatest Thing in The World by Henry Drummond*. It was a book used by Bill Wilson and Dr. Bob back in the days in Ohio when they spent time in prayer and meditation with each other. It is an analysis of love as the greatest ingredient of a person's makeup. It is still popular today and used by many people in a 12 step program. He didn't believe his young charge would really read it for some reason or another so he appealed to his ego. He told him of his love for the book and really would appreciate it if he would read and record it for him to keep. He told him his voice was so wonderful and no one else could be considered to make this important recording. Of course, the man was anxious to impress with his wonderful voice and thus read the book.

One last example of the love people in this fellowship share, although I could write a separate book on all the examples of it. My Father always went to retreats for people in the program. A retreat is a weekend in an area, sometimes a monastery, sometimes retreat houses. A visiting priest or nun who is in the program leads a weekend of meetings, usually based on a spiritual aspect of the program. My Father usually attended at least three a year.

As his health declined with age he remained as active as ever in the program. Although he was in his eighties he still had a swarm of young men who loved being with him and with whom he shared his knowledge, experience and love for the program.

The last retreat he wanted to attend looked doubtful as his failing health made travel and staying in a room by himself unlikely. A strapping young man who was being sponsored by my Father was going to attend this retreat also. When he learned my Father was not going to be able to go, he came and took him to this retreat.

He also slept with my Father on the inside of the bed while he slept on the outside so my Father wouldn't fall out of bed or wander in the night. He stayed by his side the whole weekend. That is the result of a love this world is so in need of. That is what a 12 step program lived in one's life can and should bring.

I hope I have whetted your imagination or desire to investigate further what the end result of a life lived in a 12 step program is meant to inspire.

One word really sums it up. **Love.** Love for a Higher Power, Love for self, Love for one another, Love for your fellowman.

The very reason one goes to a 12 step program gets swallowed up in the real activity of loving and giving and sharing and being of utmost service to one's fellowman.

<u>My Utmost for His Highest</u>

Step 11 uses the example of the prayer of St. Francis.

"Lord, make me a channel of thy peace- that where there is hatred, I may bring love- that where there is wrong, I may bring the spirit of forgiveness- - that where there is discord,

I may bring harmony- that where there is error, I may bring truth- that where there is doubt,

I may bring faith- that where there is despair, I may bring hope- that where there are shadows, I may bring light- that where there is sadness, I may bring joy. Lord, grant that I may seek rather to comfort than to be comforted- to understand, than to be understood- to love, than to be loved. For it is by self-forgetting that one finds. It is by forgiving that one is forgiven. It is by dying that one awakens to Eternal Life. Amen"

CHAPTER 5

LOOK TO THIS DAY

Relying on God has to begin all over again every day as if
nothing had yet been done.
C.S. Lewis

Perhaps one of the great reasons for the success of the 12 steps for so many different problems that are found under the umbrella of 12 step programs, is the fact that the most important day of your life is the one you are living in.

The art of living *in the now* is almost a lost art. The frenzy for the tomorrows and tomorrows that so many never get to experience are evident in the numerous ways and means that people use to try to incorporate a meaningful life into their existence. The success of television guru's uttering nothing more than common sense and television evangelists promoting spirituality at a price where they will pray for you, all point to a desperate need to make a connection on a level deeper than one is finding in their life. Self-help books are on the list of so many top sellers as people try to change and redirect their lives according to a person who you don't really know personally.

I want to change my life...tomorrow.

In Arizona several people paid very good money to experience a spiritual experience through a sweat lodge, an Indian ritual. The leader was not an Indian but he had written a book on experiencing spirituality through the practice of this Indian ritual. Several people died as a result of not properly venting the tepee used to replicate the Indian sweat lodge. People go to great lengths and expense to experience a deeper meaning and spiritual experience in their lives. They are not alone.

The idea of living in and experiencing the very moment that you are occupying is not a new one. To be present where you are and who you are with is to experience the reality of life. The only time and space you can possibly occupy is the very present moment you are in. An expression I heard many years ago was, "plan for the future, live for the day." This frees me from the unnecessary worry for the future. Insurance in place - plans for the vacation done. All-important paperwork filed and stored. An appointment book or calendar with important dates written in, with the date and time that I plan to be there. All of these preparations, done at the proper time, leave me free to be in the actual moment I am experiencing.

How many moments in life I have missed? The most intimate of experiences with my loved ones because I was preoccupied with thoughts of a later time and the elusive tomorrows?

The concept of the 12 step program is all I have is today. Yesterday is history and tomorrow is a mystery, but every day well lived will make my yesterday a day I do not regret.

The Al-anon program uses the Sanskrit prayer in the front of their manual. It is well worth repeating as a daily practice of trying to be in the actual moment that you are in. It is ageless as is the experience of living in the moment for a purposeful life.

Sanskrit Proverb

By Kalidasa

Look To This Day

For it is life,

The very life of life.

In its brief course lie all
The realities and verities of existence,
The bliss of growth,
The splendor of action,
The glory of power...

For yesterday is but a dream,
And tomorrow is only a vision.
But today, well lived,
Makes every yesterday a dream of
happiness
and every tomorrow a vision of
hope.
Look well, therefore, to this day.

Read and reread this simple truth because all everyone has is the moment we are in. By letting go of tomorrow, we may get to experience the joy we miss by not being in the moment that is within our grasp. The now!

At a retreat for families and friends of AA they explained the prayer used by the 12 step program. The serenity prayer:

God, grant me the serenity to accept the things I cannot change. The courage to change the things I can and the wisdom to know the difference.

What can't I change? I cannot change the truth, the past or you. That leaves me all day to work on the only thing I can change, myself.

The secret again is, just for this day will I try to experience the reality of this day. For just this day, I will not regret yesterday or worry about tomorrow. I will experience what is present in the here and now.

To let go of the guilt and shame of my yesterdays is like letting go of a thousand pound burden. Realizing all I can do is the best I can today. The reality of changing your life is like having a clean slate. This is the day that you can write on your slate what you want it to be. You have a brand new chance to start on the life *today* you want it to be. It is the freedom to let go of the very thing you cannot change, the past.

My Father used to say everyone is writing the story of their life. Today is the page you are living. If your life were to end on this page, what would you want it to say?

Chapter 6

WHO ARE YOU TO SAY
THERE IS NO GOD?

The brilliance of the 12 step program was recognizing that God is not a concept. God is an experience. In order to come to terms with something greater then oneself Bill Wilson understood it would have to be a God *of one's own understanding.*

Needing a spiritual solution, as Carl Jung advised that the thirst of the alcoholic was really a spiritual thirst; the problem was how to present a solution everyone could use no matter what religious persuasion they were. He needed an idea that could work for the person who hadn't had a relationship with anything or anyone, except with alcohol, for a long time.

Remember whatever your problem, overeating, gambling, drugs etc. you will need to have a spiritual solution to overcome that specific problem. It is the equivalent of math in your life. It is subtraction of the thing that is ruling, consuming and ruining your life and the addition of a spiritual solution that makes it possible to live one day at a time in peace.

By seeking your own experience with a Power greater than yourself and in turn greater than your addiction, you find your own path to freedom.

For as many people that are in any 12 step program, that is how many different concepts you will find of a Higher Power. They are all valid and they all work. Bill Wilson noted that God does not make too hard of terms for those who seek Him.

One problem that many encounter as they embark on a journey of living one day at a time in a spiritual solution is the idea that because they have been so bad in their own addiction, they must be the catalyst that makes themselves good, in order to experience a relationship with a Power greater then themselves. It is the need to be doing something. It is so hard to relax and believe that by the addition of something greater than oneself you have actually done enough to start. It is the Power that will make the change that you have been unable to.

In other words it is not in trying harder but in surrendering more.

The addiction is always a panacea for a problem that already exists. In almost every case when a solution is found albeit alcohol, eating, gambling, sex, etc., it immediately gives us an answer for resolving some inner conflict in our lives. For the addict, the solution is also the very thing that at first solves a problem and then creates a problem more serious than the one it first resolved. The solution becomes the problem and all the other things we thought we had escaped rush back and seem more hopeless. We are now the slaves and the solution is the master.

What I saw in my Father and his friends was a way of living that had changed them from character to character until they no longer resembled their former selves. They lost the need to please and instead gave pleasure. They didn't seek approval, they gave approval. They weren't needy for attention and love they gave attention and love. They became in almost all instances the living prayer of Saint Francis. They had walked through the archway into a way of living that gave them the freedom to be real. They were loved and they reflected that love back to one another. They cared more for the welfare of each other than seeking their own welfare first. Bill Wilson described it as the language of the heart.

By entering a 12 step program you have admitted that something in your life was out of control and causing enough pain that you were seeking a solution. (Step 1)

At step 2 you realized, left on your own devices, that you were unable to stop the behavior that was causing so much pain. Although you were rational in every other aspect, when it came to this one thing you saw it ruled your life.

At step 3, you give up on trying to control behavior and turn instead to turning your living and thinking over to something or someone greater than yourself. You quit trying harder and surrender to the fact that you need outside help.

The program will include people at various stages of surrender. What they become are powers of attraction. You realize they have the very same symptom that is killing you but they have found a way to live, one day at a time,

subtracting the thing harming them and adding a
Power to help them through the day with peace.
A peace that is so powerful, you actually wish
for that peace more than the thing that is
harming you.

Step 4 is an inventory into your life to
find out why you have chosen a solution that
harms rather than helps you. All people find
ways to cope with life. They find a solution
when things are not ideal and they never are.
They find an answer that helps them to manage
an unmanageable life. Some people find it in
food. Food gives them comfort and when life
hands them a problem they placate the problem
with food. Some people escape into a world
where the brain doesn't need to be engaged.
Gambling and video games do the trick. They
help you to flee into a world where you can
escape feelings of inadequacies and
powerlessness. Drugs and alcohol usually give
the person using them a feeling of power and
superiority. It fills them with the ability to
escape into a world where they are everything
they know they are not. Some people seek titles
and education. Always more titles and education
as though they can fill a void in their life
with accomplishments on the wall, that don't

fill their souls. Some people seek to work constantly; it is a way to have control in a life that is out of control on the inside.

All people have their panacea and never have a problem. The ones who seek help are the addictive personalities. These are the people who endanger their lives with selfish behavior. They are the ones who ignore all requests from loved ones to alter their behavior. They are the ones who may face divorce and exclusion from families rather than change their dangerous behavior. They are victims of the idea that they cannot give up the very thing that gives them a solution to life because they have nothing else to replace it. Since I have seen these steps work on the worst case scenarios, I am convinced they can help anyone seeking to add something to their own life.

Prayer of a long dead slave.

Lord I ain't what I want to be.

I ain't what I ought to be and

I ain't what I'm gonna be,

But thanks Lord I ain't what I used to be.

THE STORIES

Each story is by an anonymous contributor.

He who finds a thought

that enables him

to obtain a slightly deeper glimpse

into the eternal secrets

of his nature

has been given a great grace.

Albert Einstein

Mena

"I didn't realize alcohol was putting a Band-Aid
on an emptiness within"

I grew up in a big crazy Italian family. I was constantly surrounded by loving family members and great food. I learned early on that if I wanted to be heard I had to be loud. I felt like I had to do great things to rise above the noise. I have a brother two years older than me. He was constantly getting in trouble and school teachers always would ask me if I was going to be like him. I would always respond with, "no I'm the good one", and I played that part well.

When I was eight my mom had my little brother, then three sisters followed him. At that time I was not too excited to share the attention with all these new additions but I later found them to be a wonderful distraction that helped me to live my double life.

Being an Italian family wine at dinner was a usual thing and I always loved when I was able to have a sip. I started sneaking more and

44

more booze at family parties and a few times had to be carried to the car by an embarrassed mother and father. I can remember when I was 15, Italy won the world cup and everyone was so happy they didn't notice me stealing all their drinks. My cousin, who was just two years older than me and my partner in crime, was trying to show me how to throw up so we wouldn't get too drunk in front of the family. I couldn't comprehend why she would want to make that amazing feeling go away.

In the book Alcoholics Anonymous there is a sentence that states "Men and woman drink essentially because they like the effect produced by alcohol" For me, this sentence has great importance. Alcohol made me feel powerful and in control.

I've heard people say that even before they started drinking they felt different or apart from everyone else and I'm no exception. I always felt like I was better or somehow older than people my own age but a step behind my older cousin and her friends. I always felt like I needed to act older than what I was. Whether it was to help out with my younger brother and sisters or I had to be good to lessen the stress of my older brother always being in trouble. Drinking was my way to be who I wanted to be and not what I felt people expected me to be.

I started blacking out my sophomore year of high school. Every weekend I would drink as much as possible and during the week I would work after school and play sports. My mother was very protective of me and always made sure to check everywhere I was going to be and call parents before I slept over. Luckily for me I made friends with girls whose parents drank and would lie to my mother. During the week I was a hardworking athlete and attended an all-girl's Catholic school and volunteered to teach catholic education once a week. But on the weekend I was a party animal. I fell under my parents' radar most of the time as they were busy with the younger children. But on those few occasions I did get caught they would direct my attention to my older brother and his transgressions.

Before I went off to college my older brother went into rehab and I can remember thinking he was so stupid for messing up and not being able to drink anymore. Because of him I never did any type of pills or hard drugs because I didn't want to get sent to rehab as well. Alcohol was all I ever needed anyway. With my brother away my mother started to notice my drinking and questioned me more. I always told her she was crazy and was just trying to lump me in with my brother and she believed me.

When I went off to an out of state college all bets were off. I didn't have to have anyone's parents lie for me so I could drink. I could drink every day of the week if I wanted to, so I did. I missed countless classes and blacked out so many times my roommates started to worry about me. I ended up having to leave that college and come back home to go to a college near my house. I got an apartment with some girls and continued my drinking. Because I was close by my mother she began to notice my drinking and worry. She convinced me to see a therapist to find out if something was bothering me. I, of course, lied to the therapist about almost everything.

I do remember telling her that I don't understand why I drink so much since nothing in my life was going wrong in my eyes. I had a loving family, a job, a car, and the attention of any boy if I wanted it. For some reason though drinking was on my mind constantly. She was never able to tell me why I drank. I ended up getting too drunk before an appointment with the therapist never went back.

Near the end of my drinking, alcohol didn't make me feel powerful or in control anymore. When I started to drink I started to feel hatred for myself and it scared me. I would sit in my room alone and drink and cry, or I would be around people and I would be violent. My roommate who had been my best friend since first grade called me an alcoholic and next thing I knew I came to with my knee on her neck punching her in the face. Before blacking out was an accident, near the end blacking out became deliberant. I had to drink as fast as possible so I wouldn't feel the suicidal thoughts or remember anything. One afternoon I woke up with bruises all over, my mattress off the bed frame and a bunch of missed calls from my mother. Still drunk I texted her that I couldn't stop drinking. And I wanted to die. Next thing I knew I had a plane ticket to come to Arizona and I was set to leave in less than a week. I suspect she may have been waiting for me to ask for help.   Unfortunately I didn't make it to rehab that next week.

Knowing I was not going to be able to drink in rehab I had to make sure I got good and drunk before I left. The day before my plane was to take off I got drunk and drove my car off the road into a ditch. Two boys found me bleeding out in the backseat of my car with a broken back, pelvis, several broken ribs, and my head split open at the top. My mother nursed me back to health and as soon as I could walk I snuck down into the wine cellar to steal wine from her. I can vividly remember my last drink. I was laying in bed in pain from my car accident and I had two bottles of wine I had taken from the cellar. As I drank them I thought about how I was no longer the fun party girl and that I better chug the drinks fast so I could pass out.

I thought that once I stopped drinking everything would just fall into place. I believed myself to be a smart and capable person who just drank a little too much. Unfortunately for me once I put the bottle down things got worse. I didn't realize alcohol was putting a band aid on the emptiness within me and without it I started to feel how large that hole was. I turned to the next best thing for me which was the attention of men. I went from obsessing about alcohol to obsessing over every guy that walked my way. I saw other people doing the steps and praying and finding God but I felt like I didn't have to work as hard as them plus I needed to find a boyfriend.

I had known God my whole life, through church and my family. I had no problem acknowledging He existed I just wasn't going to ask Him for much direction. It wasn't until I was 14 months completely sober that I found myself in more pain and loneliness that I ever felt before. I didn't understand why nothing could make me happy and the thought of suicide returned. I ended up in a mental institution for a very brief period and when I got out I ran to my sponsor. I can remember sitting in a park with her and I was crying and for the first time in a long time, I humbly asked "what do I do?" My sponsor told me I needed to run to God and I did.

I finally learned that I didn't have all the answers and I needed someone to help run my life. I didn't really know how to start turning my life over to God I was expecting some weird ceremony then poof I was going to be cured and hear God all the time. Instead my sponsor had pointed out to me though I have believed in God my whole life the perception I had of Him was off. I found that I saw God as vindictive and spiteful. I thought He would punish me if I didn't pray enough or go to church. I also gave God human qualities. I felt that he was too busy with everyone else to listen to my prayers so I would have to continue taking care of everything myself. My sponsor pointed out to me I don't trust most people so why would I turn my life over to someone who didn't have time to listen to me and was going to punish me at every turn. At that moment I had to start building my own idea of God. That didn't mean I had to get rid of the God I grew up with from childhood, instead I just had to make Him more personal to me.

I chose to use my mother as a basis to start. I knew my mother loved me more than anything and all she wanted was the best for me and for me to be happy. I decided to make love the focal point of my new perception of God. I could start to give my life over to something I knew loved me and was looking out for me. As I continued through my steps and cleaned up my past I have been able to let God be more and more into my life, my journey to trust God has had many ups and downs. It's not always easy to trust God to take care of me. When things go wrong my first instinct is to go into survivor mode and handle everything myself. I have to constantly look back at all the things I've been through and see the evidence of God taking care of me all along. There are times when I talk to Him all the time and can't stop thanking Him for all the good He has given me. And then there are times were I can go days without praying. The difference for me now is I'm never scared to go back to Him. I no longer think if I miss a few days praying that God will no longer listen to me because my God provides me with grace. That empty feeling has slipped away entirely. I have a life more amazing than I could even ask for. I have a great relationship with my family, friends that love me for me and a healthy relationship with a man I love. God has allowed me to find contentment and serenity. I'm no longer searching for something outside to make me feel better or fill that hole because God has filled it for me.

Courtney's Story

"The only thing left to do was

To die or get help"

Like many of us who have some sort of addiction, I grew up in somewhat of an unstable environment. My father was an alcoholic. He was a daily drinker with short stints of sobriety throughout my childhood. While I always felt loved, I also always felt afraid, afraid that my father was going to drink again.

Unfortunately my mom had no one to talk to so she talked to me as an adult which was pretty heavy stuff for a child to process. Sometime during my childhood I got the idea that I always had to be good, that I could not fail. I felt so different from my peers. I felt less-than. I had to achieve more, do things bigger to make up for feeling inadequate.

I made it through my high school years for the most part un-phased. I was the kid who smoked weed, drank, did other drugs, but at the same time was involved with school clubs and events. There was a side of me who knew I wanted to have a successful life, but there was also that side that didn't feel good enough, which may be why I chose to hang with the bad kids too. I scraped by in high school not getting good grades, but did well enough to graduate. I knew that I wanted to go to college, so I attended a community college until my grades were good enough to get into a university. I worked really hard and finally was accepted to college. I think that is when my disease of perfectionism began to set in. For the first time in my life, I felt smart. I began to place my value on what I did and the praise on got from others. I never truly valued myself for the person I was. I had very low self-esteem.

During college, when I was 21, I experienced my first episode of depression. I had no idea what was happening to me. I did not know how to cope or deal, so I just pretended for six long months that everything was ok. I began to drink a lot at that time, however when the depression lifted, I went back to just drinking socially. I think that was just a preview into my alcoholism. It was one of the darkest, scariest times of my life. Not a place I ever wanted to go back to, but unfortunately I found myself there again two years later.

My second episode of depression kicked in after I graduated college. This time I sought the help of a psychiatrist. I was very low and could not eat or sleep. Anxiety was a huge component of my depression. My doctor prescribed me an anxiety medication. He told me to take them as needed. But being the addict I was, unbeknownst to me at the time, I needed them constantly. They worked and I felt better, so I why wouldn't I take them every day, all day. That is an addict's thinking. People actually took these things as needed. I couldn't believe it! It took no time to become highly addicted to this medication.

For the next few years I was able to have a successful career as a journalist, still addicted to my anxiety medication. In order to keep up with my addiction, I would see multiple doctors at a time, without them knowing. I had multiple prescriptions going at once. I did whatever it took to get my pills. I would sit in emergency rooms for hours to get a prescription and I always did because addicts become very good at manipulation and I was one of the best. It didn't take long until that soul sickness kicked in to the point where it was hard to ignore. I did not feel fulfilled, happy, content, or good enough. I was extremely depressed. The pills stopped working. I was always searching for something to make me feel whole - when this happens, I will be happy or when I achieve this, I will be happy. I began to drink and additionally became highly addicted to pain medication. This led me to my bottom which fortunately happened quickly.

I was at the jumping off point they talk about in the big book of Alcoholics Anonymous. I had lost my job, alienated myself from most friends and family, burned many bridges and was so depressed I didn't know how to go on. I ran out of money, resources and the only thing left to do was die or get help. I sought help in many ways, I tried many gimmicks, read self-help books and saw many therapists. It wasn't until I saw the last therapist that I knew what I had to do. He told me he could not treat me until I detoxed. He said, "You are an addict and you need help." I felt relieved. There was a reason my life had fallen apart and there might be an answer. For the first time in a long time, I felt hopeful. I packed for rehab a week later.

I called my mom and told her what my therapist had said. My mom said she was already looking into rehab centers for me and gave me a number to call. I called. They said they didn't have any beds available but to keep calling. I was on a waiting list and was so desperate to get in, I called a couple of times a day. A bed finally opened and I jumped in with both feet, hopeful to get myself and my life back. I was sort of naive to the process. I thought I would simply detox for ten days and when the pills were out of my system, I would feel like me again. That was so far from reality. I didn't realize how sick I really was.

The pills were my coping mechanism, the only one I knew. When they were stripped away, I was left with me, all of the same character defects and nothing to take the place of the pills. I was terrified. While I was in rehab, several groups brought Alcoholics Anonymous and Narcotics Anonymous meetings in. I was told in rehab if I wanted to stay sober, I could, and my answer was the program of Alcoholics Anonymous. I also attended Narcotics Anonymous and Pills Anonymous, but Alcoholics Anonymous became my home. I went to my first meeting out of rehab. I remember people looking healthy and happy. There were also those quivering in the corner, myself included, so I didn't feel completely like a fish out of water. I remember telling a women that I just got out of rehab. She gave me a big hug. I remember how warm she was and how sincere her hug felt. That women became my sponsor.

Feeling so uncomfortable in my own skin and desperate for relief, I jumped right into the steps. I don't know why God gave me the sponsor he did, but I will forever be grateful to him for it. She had everything to do with my positive introduction into Alcoholics Anonymous. I spent every Saturday with her for the next year. She became my family. We worked the steps and went to lunch and I would just run errands with her. She was so content and at peace, I wanted what she had. She would always tell me the relief is in the steps and I found that it was.

While working the steps, the shame of my past lessened. I began to gain more self-esteem. More importantly, I found God and that is when my life began to change. The craving was lifted and I learned how to turn my crazy thinking over to God. I surrendered and for the first time in a long time, I felt content, even happy. I attended a meeting pretty much every day my first year. All of my friends were in AA and we took AA very seriously. We would do service work together, bring meetings to hospitals and institutions and we would talk AA all of the time. I was actually having fun without having to put a substance in my body. I was able to get out of bed and start my day without self-medicating. I had new meaning. I found a place where I didn't have to pretend to be ok.

Months had gone by and I felt confident enough to go back to work. I went right back into my career and who knew! I could do my job without pills and I was even better at it! I was responsible and loyal and I actually did what I said I was going to do. My friendships were deeper and real and full of substance. I loved my new life in AA and it felt good to be working and contributing. I worked very hard and had multiple promotions. While working I continued my program, going to meetings and doing service work. A few years later, I entered the next phase of my life.

I met my future husband. This was the healthiest and happiest relationship I had ever been in and I owe it all to the program of AA. We were married and began to start a family. We

had a beautiful, healthy boy and a girl. I
always heard people say your life would become
better than you could ever imagine for yourself
as long as you stay sober. At the time, I
thought it was BS, because I felt so awful
early on, but it was true. My life was
beautiful and I felt so blessed for it. I also
heard people say, life still happens; the
difference is we now have a solution.

Life definitely happened for me. I was
diagnosed with multiple sclerosis a few years
into sobriety. A couple of years after that, I
had my son and suffered severe post-partum
depression. This was the first time in sobriety
where my program and my faith in God were
tested. The depression and anxiety got so bad,
I checked myself into a behavior health
hospital. I was terrified. I learned that no
matter how good my program was and how
spiritually fit I was, that sometimes it's not
enough. When the dark cloud of depression is
over you, it is hard to feel God. At least that
was the case for me.

I relied heavy on my friends in AA. I had
an amazing group of women who carried me
through this dark time. I thought about
drinking and using pills many times and always

shared about it in meetings. I believe that took some of the power out of it. I also got post-partum depression with my daughter. It was the hardest three years of my life. My belief in God was tested. I was mad at Him and many times wondered if He even existed. It was dark and lonely, but I got through it, and I got through it sober. I learned that as long as I stay close to the program and don't drink or use, I could probably get through anything.

Today my life is beautiful. I have been beaten and bruised in sobriety, but I am still sober. Most of the time, I am happy and content. I get to raise my children as a sober mother. My kids nor my husband have seen me drunk or high and God willing they never will. "Life still happens" and I am not perfect nor will I ever be, but I am present and a participant in my own life. I am blessed beyond measure and am incredibly grateful.

Alicia

"This is what it means to be the change you want to see in the world."

I was recently meandering through a wonderful local farmer's market when I stumbled upon the most delightful booth. The vendor made beautiful vintage jewelry. As I combed over all of the pieces, there it was! Jumping right out from the rows was a leather wrap bracelet with a large metal piece of hardware that simply said "48". To most people, that might mean nothing at all, but to me, it meant everything. It was a direct message from God that I am right where I am supposed to be, that He is watching over me, that He hears me, and that nothing in my life today is by mistake, but rather all according to His better plan.

"48", also known as 4848 South Central in Phoenix, is where I got sober just over 8 years ago. It is the first meeting of Alcoholics Anonymous that I ever attended and I've never had a drink since. One of my best friends I met at my very first AA meetings. That was the day that my life began. Some people say that when they got sober they got their life back, but I say it is when mine began because I would not want any part of my alcoholic life back. Today my life is full and beautiful. Yes, it has its challenges and I still struggle from time-to-time with my emotional sobriety or feelings of anxiety, but those times pass quickly as I move closer to God and they are small stints in time versus a way of life. My worst day sober is still better than my best day drinking.

I grew up in a small town in Kansas. I often joke that one of the "things to do" was to drive around and drink beer. It was an actual pastime. However, I was always the hero child growing up, which meant I got straight A's, had a job, played sports, and was responsible and respectful. I know I tried beer in high school, but it was uneventful enough that I don't remember my first drink. I do remember that I was too afraid of displeasing my parents to overindulge. I do remember being somewhat of a loaner in high school and not every feeling like I fit in. I was uncomfortable in my skin and felt very out-of-place.

I graduated from high school and set off for The University of Kansas. Having grown up leading a sheltered life, I was in for a big shock. After settling in to my new dorm room, some girls started to befriend me. I was invited out the first night to "party". I had no idea what I was in for, but I was excited that someone wanted to hang out with me and it felt really good to be free!! Not having parents to answer to helped me relax into the idea of "finding myself". That first night out I found alcohol. I got black-out drunk and I felt things I'd never felt before. I felt empowered, cool, confident, pretty, rebellious, invigorated, and courageous, I finally felt like I fit in. I thought I'd found myself, but I found a lot more than I ever bargained for.

Somehow I managed to get good grades and hold down 2 jobs in college, all while partying 5-6 nights per week. I know where all the drink specials were and I rarely left a bar without being extremely drunk. I never thought I had a problem, I just thought I was young and having fun. Despite waking up in places I didn't recognize with people I didn't know and forgetting entire periods of time, I felt I had things under control and I was loving all my friends and the exciting and fun life I was leading.

I graduated and took a job just outside of Denver, Colorado. I was finally a full adult with my own job, my own money and my own ideas about the world. In Colorado, I began to find more than just alcohol. It was there that I began to experiment with marijuana and ecstasy. Despite having a career, my partying did not slow down. I was out multiple nights a week, dancing on bars, smoking pot, taking ecstasy and still doing all the same things as before. A bad relationship motivated me to move yet again. I thought if I transferred with my company to somewhere I knew no one that I could start fresh and reinvent myself. I hopped in a Penske truck and headed for the hottest place I could find, Phoenix, Arizona.

My life was only calmer for about 5 minutes in Phoenix. They say "birds of a feather flock together", that was absolutely true for me. I immediately got connected with other people who partied like me and I quickly expanded my repertoire to include cocaine. What an amazing drug I had found! I could snort cocaine and be more alert than I was with alcohol and I could drink more and party longer. I began to seek out coke very regularly, even buying it for myself from time-to-time. And so the story goes...I drank more, partied harder, and my life got crazier. I had several relationships spattered throughout this time. At one point I was involved with a police officer. He often worked nights, so I would take advantage of the ability to party when he was working. One night, I got so drunk that I took my car around a corner at 60 miles per hour and hit a sign and severely damaged my car. I managed to hide it in a parking lot and call him for help. I told the insurance company I'd hit a deer and never endured a consequence. It never occurred to me that the drinking was the problem. I just moved right along as if nothing had ever happened.

There were many near misses for me, but finally, at 25 I was arrested for a DUI. I hired an excellent attorney and got it plead down to reckless driving, but I had to spend 10 days in the infamous "Tent City". It was a terrifying, humbling, eye opening experience. While I was in jail, I began for one of the first times, to reflect on my drinking. I made up my mind that I was finished with alcohol.

When I got released I didn't touch alcohol for 4 months. I white knuckled it for sure. I basically shut myself off from friends and life because I didn't know how else to not drink.

After 4 months without alcohol, I decided it was time to date. One night I went on a first date with a man and he was very curious why I did not drink. I just kept saying I didn't want to. After enough pressure and convincing, I was off to the races again. I got black out drunk that night. I remember being terrified because I didn't feel entirely comfortable with him, but I didn't want to drive home and get another DUI. He offered to follow me home to make sure that no cops got behind me and pulled me over. At the time, my impaired brain told me that was a great idea. When we got to my house he asked me to use my restroom and I obliged. As he came out I was walking around the corner and he grabbed me and threw me down and raped me. That was one of the darkest periods of my life because of the intense self-loathing that I felt. I felt that if I hadn't been so drunk, I wouldn't have let that happen. I blamed myself not only for the assault, but I felt absolute shame and demoralization for having given in to drinking.

It was then that my drinking began to change and escalate. I was afraid of drinking out in public settings because I didn't want to get a DUI or be assaulted again, so I started drinking at home alone to numb the pain. I started seeing a therapist, but unfortunately I manipulated her to teach me how to drink and then I lied to her about how much I'd been drinking and pretended I had been staying within her limits. I call those my $100 lies. I was drinking more and withdrawing from society more.

I met another man and moved to Tucson for a relationship. The man I got involved with drank like me, so we were a match made in heaven. On our second date we drank five bottles of wine together. We drank every night and even sometimes during the day. I often changed my drink from wine to beer to try and get less drunk or to tequila and vitamin water because it was "healthy" in my delusional mind. I knew at that point, alcohol had its hooks in me! I was experiencing the daily obsession of my mind that I had to drink to experience the ease and comfort that comes with it. I was also experiencing the phenomenon of craving! Once I put liquor in my body, I had to have more. I didn't know what would happen and I couldn't control my drinking. Somehow, I'd managed to perform in my career, get an MBA, and make an excellent income despite my secret alcohol problem. Everything looked great on the outside. I had the designer clothes, the fancy car, the houses, the trips, the boyfriend and the high profile job, but inside I was an absolute slave, totally being dominated by liquor.

It didn't take long for me to sabotage yet another relationship and move again. I moved back to Phoenix heartbroken and totally lost. Every time I moved I thought I could reinvent myself, but every time I picked up where I left off. The situation was no different when I moved back to Phoenix. I was a daily drinker, alone at home with few friends and not much of a life. I was depressed, and I was an empty shell of a human being. I was totally devoid of any spirituality and I thought the world was to blame for all of my problems. I was lacking any and all accountability and the fact that I had a part in anything was a very foreign concept. I was at my bottom and it was at that point that God ransomed me.

While traveling for work, I decided to go to a local book store one evening to find something to read while I drank my wine. I stumbled upon two books. "Act Like a Lady, Think Like a Man" and "The Shack". I didn't really care if there was a God or not and all talk of God made me uncomfortable, so I shied away from "The Shack". However, I knew men and dating were my true problem, so I couldn't wait to read the other book! After walking around the store, I kept coming back to "The Shack". Finally, I picked it up and bought it as if it were a force bigger than me making me do it. It took a few weeks, but I finally was open to the idea of reading "The Shack" since it was after all, a book about God.

What happened was truly a miracle. I read the book and I began to believe that maybe there was something bigger than me out there. I began to wonder if I'd been shying away from the idea of God because I thought I had to "be" something specific to have God approve of me. Since I knew I would fail at "being" what I thought God wanted me to "be", I went the opposite way of not caring at all. It was only when my eyes were opened to the fact that God simply wanted a personal relationship with me and was happy to meet me wherever I was at, that things began to change. I pondered this concept for two weeks and God took over.

Sunday September 7, 2009 was a day like any other. Except, this Sunday, I decided after two weeks of thinking about this God concept that I would attend church with some family members. I joined them at their church and a song was played that said "when all the lights in the world are out his light still shines on you". I became very emotional and cried. I FELT for the first time, the presence of God. I went on to have a normal day and upon returning home at 5 PM the thought came to me that I should make a drink. There, in that moment is the unmanageability. No matter if a day was bad or good, emotional or emotionless; everything was a reason to drink. I had lost the power of choice. Even with some God consciousness, I NEEDED to drink. So I began to drink the leftovers from Friday night's debauchery. After several drinks, while sitting alone on my patio, the thought came to me, "I have a drinking problem. This is my problem. Alcohol is my problem". The moment of clarity had arrived and today I firmly believe that was God doing for me what I could not do for myself.

I started calling friends. I got two people on the phone. One friend suggested I stop drinking. I thought she was nuts! Why would I not get good and drunk if this was to be my last hoorah! The second person I called was my brother's wife. She was not a friend, but I believe it was preordained that I would call her because she had suggested AA to me before and she would hold me accountable. The next morning I woke up from a drunken blackout once again suffering from incomprehensible demoralization. Within minutes my phone rang and it was my brother's wife. At this point I was very much regretting having called her. I was beginning to already have thoughts that it was a mistake and I didn't want to quit drinking. This is the insanity of drinking. Alcoholism is a disease of thinking more than drinking. It is an illness that takes a hold of the mind of the alcoholic and fills it with falsehoods. It is an allergy of the body that causes the alcoholic to react differently than his fellows to the poison of alcohol.

My brother's wife asked me to come over. I reluctantly did in the humiliated fashion

which I had grown accustomed to. When I
arrived they sat me down to listen to me and
then handed me a Big Book and a phone number.
I went home and started reading the book and
immediately felt a sense of calm wash over me.
I related to every word I read. I knew as I
read those words that alcohol was my problem.
The phone number was to a woman who was a sober
member of Alcoholics Anonymous. God gave me
the gumption to call her. It's amazing what
you will do when you are desperate. She told
me to hold on for a couple days and that she
would pick me up Wednesday and take me to a
women's meeting. I white knuckled it for two
nights and then Wednesday came. The woman
picked me up and I immediately felt comfortable
with her. She took me to have coffee, told me
her story, listened to mine and took me to that
meeting at 4848 South Central. I took a
ticket, stood up when my number was called and
told a bit of my story. That night I asked
that woman to be my sponsor and I've never had
another drop of alcohol.

It is amazing to watch God at work. When
the door of belief and hope are cracked open
ever so slightly, God will come flooding in.
My life got very good, very quickly. I won

Sales Rep of the Year that year. Four months after I got sober, I met my husband. It was definitely challenging to date that soon and I wouldn't recommend it, but I did and here we are. He is a normal drinker so that has presented some challenges along the way, but nothing that the principals and steps of AA and God couldn't help me overcome. We have had 3 beautiful children and have been through some very difficult times including losing our home to a fire. While life has happened on life's terms, I haven't used alcohol as a solution. There have been times that drinking was at the forefront of my mind; times I came very close to making it my solution. But for the grace of God I did not. My first sponsor told me, "I can take you through the steps, help you socially, and give you sober suggestions, but your sobriety is between you and God and at the end of the day, I can't keep you sober, only God can". I never forgot that because it is the truth. Sobriety is a gift and it is a brief daily reprieve contingent upon the maintenance of my spiritual condition. When I invite God in and surrender EVERYTHING to Him, life goes well and I stay sober. It is only when I slip back into the mindset that I can manage myself and others my way that I get into trouble. You see, I am always moving toward or away from God, but God never moves.

My focus today in sobriety is emotional sobriety. You can't really be sober unless your actions and behaviors line up with the principals of the AA program. It is very easy to not drink, but still be a tornado in the lives of others, but that is not sobriety.

Sobriety is love. Sobriety is service, kindness, humility, courage, God centered, surrender. So today, when my spouse doesn't behave how I think he should, I don't get to act out, try to win at all costs, be right, withhold love, manipulate to be rescued, or any of the other old behaviors that I feel so comfortable in. Today when people don't act how I think they should, I have to say "Thy will be done". Today, I look at myself, my part, my defects of character and I pray that God will help me to behave in my assets, to be kind, loving, tolerant, and accepting. Today, even when I'm so uncomfortable that it hurts to breathe, I pause, I pray, and I let God do God's job. Only God is big enough to change you or me. Only God knows the plan for the future. Who am I to interfere? As my sponsor says "I am a full time job". Just for today, I have to focus on me, what is wrong with me, and how I can improve me with God. That is what it means to do as Gandhi said and "be the change you want to see in the world".

STEVEN

"I am a lifer in prison"

I, like a lot of you, have tried countless attempts to skate my way through life in the most pleasurable way. Never thinking of the affect my actions would have on my victims, for the remainder of their lives, as well as for family members, and for me.

I have struggled to put my personal story in writing, hoping and praying that it will help another human being avoid the tragic lifestyle that my poor decisions, under the influence of alcohol and narcotics, has caused for me in my life.

At a very young age I got to share some marijuana with a friend who was wiser and older than I. I had a slight head change from the first four or five hits. Soon everything was magnified. I loved everything so much more. I knew smoking at my age had to be kept secret from my family. I also knew the experience I had enjoyed in that rolled up joint was something I wanted to experience again. My addictive personality was off to the races.

All I cared about was riding my bike, getting money to get more weed to smoke and experiencing that high again.

Being so young I had to pursue dishonest ways to make money, which included stealing from family, friends and local businesses.

Being young and inept I would often get caught, which entailed lectures, detentions and sometimes a beating from my friends who realized I had stolen from them. Nothing was off limits to experience the thrill that I would feel when using the "harmless" substance.

If times were really good, now and then, my friends and I would score some alcohol to go along with our adult activity of smoking a joint. These were the best of times, because no punishment could compare to the feeling of nirvana, in these stolen moments.

My parents tried every means to curb my activities but all warnings fell on deaf ears. By the time I failed eighth grade for the second time, I felt left behind. All my friends and the girls I thought I loved moved on and I was forgotten. I was the same boy who had skipped second grade and felt so superior to my peers. Looking back from third grade to eighth grade smoking marijuana had led me down a path of failure with school, my family and the law.

My life was on a spiral descending downwards. I took different hallucinatory drugs, L.S.D., magic mushrooms. I sniffed paint and typing white out, which I used to put in a baggy and sniff the chemicals out of it… anything I could - just to get high. I attributed my descent as the reason I needed to get high, not thinking that getting high was actually creating my trip into hell.

I went to many different schools, doctors, reform schools etc. Frankly, I was incorrigible. I am very ashamed of where my life and my decisions have put me today.

To make a long story shorter, as I grew up my love affair with alcohol and drugs continued.

I fell in love and married a beautiful woman. I was sure I could change for her. I was head over heels for her, but it didn't take long before I was staying out and drinking instead of being home with her. It is the love affair anyone is familiar with when one is in love with an alcoholic. It is always a triangle.

I never looked at the cost of the love affair with drugs and alcohol cost me. I only saw it as a solution for a very depressing life and a lot of bad breaks.

During one of my blackouts I was driving. All I remember is waking up in a hospital. I was told that I had been in a serious motor vehicle accident in March of 1990. I had apparently crashed the vehicle, been thrown out and rode the windshield for a long distance down the highway, exposing my head and body to velocity speed on the pavement.

I was not supposed to be alive. I was in a coma for two months. They had to drain my brain because of the swelling. I was told I would never walk again and I would be a vegetable. I was in for months of rehabilitation, just to learn basic skills again.

I made a remarkable comeback after months of therapy and I did walk with limitations. The doctors told me that because of the brain trauma, I should never use alcohol or drugs again, as I would not be able to process them properly anymore. Imagine my luck when one of the very few people I spent months in rehab with was telling me he was going to score some marijuana. Apparently having your brains spattered on a highway is not enough to forget your attraction to getting high.

I was able to get disability and began a new descent into addiction.

Eventually I lost the girl, I lost my family and I was living hand to mouth waiting for my ship to come in. I was able to secure a couple of guns and with my life style I did need protection. I was waiting for money to come in and it wasn't there fast enough for me to enjoy my pastime. I made the decision to secure the money I needed by using the gun. I was high when I made the decision and high when I committed armed robbery. Not everyone made it home that night. I did. But my fate was sealed.

I hope that if you are reading my story today, you will be able to put all mind altering substances out of your life for good.

Despite my circumstances, that is just what I have done. Under the worst circumstances I have done just that, one day at a time. I have gotten my high school diploma in prison and I help other convicts get the best

education that they can here. I attend A.A. and
N.A. meetings. I also chair them and console
any who comes here via the route I took. It is
never too late. My life is now drug and alcohol
free…in the worst situation but I am freer than
I ever have been compared to when I was outside
these walls. God is alive and active inside
Florence State Prison walls.

My Mother and Father have both passed away
while I am incarcerated here but I am connected
to them on a spiritual level now. I know they
are proud of the decisions I have made behind
bars. I also have lost many family members and
have to mourn them in the silence of my cell.
But being able to handle life on life's terms
in the worst of conditions has made me aware
that I am the man they always wanted me to be.

Jamie

"To thine own self be true"

Why do we ask everyone we know what they would do in our circumstances? We tend to keep on asking until we get the answer we are looking for. If that someone hasn't had the experiences we have had, then they are giving us misinformation, and we don't listen. If that someone can relate to our experiences, we *trust* them and listen to that advice. Our stories can be so different, but we can find solutions by working the steps to change our attitudes and accept that we are exactly where we need to be. We have to experience that which make us stronger, that which we can pass to another person for healing. No suffering goes unused.

The steps are a spiritual journey that take us through healing obsessions of the mind and allow us the joys we are meant to experience. Faith and control can't peacefully co-exist, so we let go of control, believe in a power greater than ourselves and alter our perception for the better.

I need to first be ok with myself, before I can be myself with another person.

I was second from the oldest, in a family of eight. I had always felt like the black sheep of the family. I never felt that I fit in, even though I was popular in school, great at sports and excelled in academics. I had an obsession in my head that told me I wasn't worthy and I hid behind the façade of my popularity.

There was physical abuse in my childhood and at the age of thirteen I had feelings of being gay. In the early 70's, I didn't even know what it was called to love someone of the same sex. So for years, I had secrets and was good at not talking about myself, lest something would slip out. I didn't want to be looked at as attractive and hid in the shadow of my three sisters. I didn't know how to tell them about myself and I didn't want them to be ashamed of me. A few times, I confided in a friend and shared my pain, only to have it used against me. So I pushed away. I put myself there….that was my survival skill.

When I was 19 years old and living on my own, I had confided in my oldest sister about

the abuse that happened as a child. Unknown to
me, she told my family and the secret was out.
I had tried to commit suicide to stop the
mental anguish that was constantly in my head.
I couldn't think of any physical pain that
would be worse than what my mind was telling
me. I remember waking up in the hospital with a
torn spleen & bladder. The realization that I
was still alive was agonizing.

When I was 24, my brother was killed by a
drunk driver. The fines then were $300 and 3
months in jail, seems so little to replace the
life of a 19 year old. That day was when I
lost my faith. That day was when I chose to be
in control and no one would take that away from
me again. I was tough at work and just as tough
in relationships….because I had to be in
control. I really never allowed people to get
close to me. When the time came and I no
longer needed them, I would end those
relationships. It seemed easier….before I was
hurt. I met someone and had a 9 year
relationship that was centered on drugs and
alcohol. When the money and trust ran out, so
did the relationship.

So I continued, not trusting. I carried my pain from relationship to relationship and wondered why I felt the way I did. I drank too much, dabbled in drugs, and became a workaholic and a perfectionist. I couldn't expose myself and felt that I was living in the bondage of my past. I even did the geographical moves to leave the memories behind. On my 14th move in six years, I realized I couldn't run from me.

I was successful at work and did a lot of international travel with friends, but I never seemed to have a partner to share those times with. I then moved to AZ, where I met many faces, but trusted none.

After about 8 years my mom's health went downhill and I became her caregiver. I tried to juggle work with appointments and had started to get resentful that I had no life. I couldn't seem to make her happy during her four years living with me. I tried to control everything and we both got more frustrated. Mom then moved back to the east coast and my sisters shared the caretaking.

A few years ago, I met someone that I felt I could start a life with. She was creative, exciting and beautiful. I wanted to give her the moon. We moved in together shortly after one year. My heart was all in and I trusted again. As things progressed, I didn't realize that I seemed to have lost myself in our relationship. If there was a disagreement, I would just walk away and not say how I felt. I was in fear of losing her and didn't know what to say or how to say it. I wanted to fix her childhood and take away all the pain she carried. So instead of speaking up, I allowed my needs to go unnoticed. The more the distance in the relationship became, the harder I tried to fix things. It only got worse. That year my mom passed away, my dog died and the relationship ended shortly after.

That person was in the program of AA, where I was introduced to the 12 step program of Al-Anon, *for friends and family of alcoholics.* I actually started the program to understand *her* better and stayed to understand *me.* I was finally able to let go of a lot of anxiety of my past and actually felt peace when working the steps. I turned to the fellowship in the rooms and I reached out to others. They didn't give advice or criticism, they just listened and allowed me to walk through my pain. They would love me until I could love myself. We do this imperfectly, sometimes with resistance. But ultimately by surrendering, accepting and forgiving; so we can feel joy and love. The steps were what saved me.

1. We admitted we were powerless, that our lives had become unmanageable. *I had no control over my life and surrendered.*

2. Came to believe that a Power greater than ourselves could restore us to sanity. *I could be open minded to a possibility of something greater than myself*

3. Made a decision to turn our will and lives over to the care of God *as* we understood Him. *Forcing my solutions wasn't working. I need to give it away. Not by my will, but Gods will for me.*

4. Made a searching and fearless moral inventory of ourselves. *To be honest with myself to admit the behaviors of my past and what my part has been. What is my responsibility? What are my fears and resentments? I am only as sick as my secrets.*

5. Admitted to God, to ourselves, and to another human being the exact nature of our wrongs. *To be vulnerable, putting ego aside and trusting another person to share my*

*story with. To be able to free myself of
the past.*

6. Were entirely ready to have God remove all
these defects of character. Be *willing to
let go of the baggage of my past, and know
that I don't have to continue the same
behaviors into my future.*

7. Humbly asked Him to remove our
shortcomings. *As I let go of behaviors I
don't need, I can be open to find strengths
that can improve my life*

8. Made a list of all persons we had harmed,
and became willing to make amends to them
all. *To be honest about my past and list
those people that I have harmed.*

9. Made direct amends to such people except to
do so would injure them or others. *To
swallow my pride and admit my part, in the
wrongs I have done to others. I can ask
for forgiveness to start to heal those
relationships.*

10. Continued to take personal inventory and
when we were wrong promptly admitted it. *To
be aware of my behaviors and when I have
harmed someone, take immediate
responsibility.*

11. Sought through prayer and meditation to improve our conscious contact with God as we understood Him, praying only for knowledge of His will for us and the power to carry that out. *For me to seek my connection to my higher power by means of; prayer, meditation and awareness. To have true faith and be mindful of living in today.*

12. Having had a spiritual awakening as the result of these steps, we tried to carry this message, and to practice these principles in all our affairs. *I need to share my experience, strength and hope. To be able to give it away to another person.*

The faith that I lost 34 years ago when my brother passed was given back to me by an alcoholic. From the seemingly bad, came a gift. I found my perfect PEACE. I can be present in my own life today and stay out of yesterday and tomorrow.

Hi, I'm Uncle Kenny
and I have alcoholism...

*"I am the only one in human history tasked with
the job of being me"*

I'm a man of 55 years, and I have alcoholism. I do not say I'm an alcoholic anymore, because God has lifted the obsession of alcohol and drugs from me almost 24 years ago. But still to this day, 8692 days as of this writing, I still have the mind of an alcoholic. It doesn't happen often anymore, but I still can think myself into insanity, right up until I ask God to intervene, and remove the bondage of self, so that I may better do His will.

When I'm asked to speak at an AA meeting, I usually open with this bit...

*When I was a little kid I was just playin...
Happy, joyous and free... Then I grew up a
little bit, and discovered thinkin... Then I
began playin about thinkin...*

*In Church, they told me that what I was
thinkin was a sin... and I lost my innocence, and*

91

God would punish me...I began thinkin about playin, complicating playin...

Then I got to thinkin about thinkin... we call that school...   In school, they told me don't worry about God, because science will fix that...

Then I had to think most the day, far too little playin...   Then I started thinkin about playin... but rarely actually playin.

About the time I started drivin, I discovered drinkin...   I began playin at drinkin....   Then I started drinkin.   Then I started drinkin without thinkin...I went downhill when I started thinkin and drinkin.   Hit bottom soon after I started drinkin about thinkin...   I had long since ceased thinkin of God, and a 16 year spiral into hell ensued.

I was not a blackout drinker. I remember everything especially that almost every time I drank I ended up on my hands and knees vomiting. And I remember that I never asked God for anything, because I believed that He would not answer.

In my early childhood, my church spoke of a vengeful God, waiting to smite me at the first wrong thought or action. So, I lived in fear of this God. I had heard so many stories

and scriptures about God and his Son that I
believed... plus my mom said it was so! *Can't go
against mom.* About the third grade in school,
I was *diagnosed* as a genius. I discovered I
could think my way into trouble and think my
way back out again. My brain was working for
me then, and it worked for me for another
handful of years. I got this life thing God,
thanks but no thanks. But soon after I began
drinking and using, I believed that God didn't
believe in me. I wasn't even worthy of His
attention, because I paid no attention to Him
for years. I began to loathe myself for this
idea. I drove anyone away that was good and
wholesome in my life because I wasn't worthy of
these kinds of folks. A few people never gave
up on me though, even if I did my best to make
them do so. True unconditional love they
showed me.

I drank and used drugs every day I could
from 1978 to early 1994. I committed thousands
of DUI, possession, drunk in public and drug
trafficking offenses, but only ever got busted
for one.

Here's that story. January 3rd, 1994,
about 3am, I was going home from a New Year's

party. Yeah, let that sink in for a moment. I
didn't think I could make it home without
peeing my pants, so I stopped at the city park
to use the restroom. When I came out, I was
greeted by two city policemen. Their patrol
car had my car blocked in, and I noticed the
officers had already searched my car and placed
much of my contraband on the roof of the car.
They asked me if that was my car. Being the
only other car around besides the patrol car, I
thought it wise to say "Yes". Well, after the
natural course of events, I found myself cuffed
and stuffed in the back of the patrol car with
5 or 6 offenses beginning with the word felony.
From the backseat of the patrol car through the
windshield, I saw on top of my car a third of a
bottle of whiskey I had forgotten about, and I
was both mad and sad that I didn't drink it
before I got to prison. Then a tidal wave of
fear gripped me... I'm going to prison! I then
said the prayer that saved my life, "God help
me now, how am I gonna get outta this one!"

Immediately after speaking this sentence a
message cracked over the police radio, "Shots
fired, officer down, all units respond". The
two officers that were still pulling stuff from
my car stood bolt upright, wide eyed, and ran

back to their patrol car. One officer grabbed my fat ass from the back seat, stood me on my feet, took the handcuffs off and said, "Wait here!" I was stunned as I watched their tail lights vanish into the city. I stood there in shock for about 20 minutes. I wasn't obeying the police; I was in fear that God was gonna spite me with a lightning bolt! In that moment, I came to believe that God did in fact believe in me, so much so that He jeopardized an officer of the law to prove it to me. This was my Spiritual Experience.

Same day, in the evening, I had been overwhelmed by the events of the early morning, and knew I had to make a change in my life, because I now believed God wasn't going to give me another chance. About 7 pm I sat down with a bottle of whiskey, telling myself that I'm going to have just one shot, one last shot, that's it, one last shot for the rest of my life. After about an hour, I was in the backyard, on my hands and knees vomiting. Bottle empty.

The very next day I checked into a rehab hospital in San Jose, CA. January 4th, 1994, my sobriety date. I enjoyed 47 days in a 30 day program in the rehab unit.

Some are sicker than other I guess. I was in AA for three days before I knew it. See, God knows I can practice contempt prior to investigation, so he will shield me from myself while he heals me enough to accept that I'm being healed in spite of myself.

Thank God for those folks that did H&I work back then. I saw in them hope. I saw in them happy, joyous and free. They couldn't be alcoholics like me; they didn't have blood or vomit on their shirts like I had. They had nice clothes and cars with current registration and everything. But they told me their stories, and told me mine at the same time, and to a man, they ALL spoke of a God of their own understanding, and how their God does for them what they could not do for themselves.

I did the twelve steps and the twelve traditions with a sponsor. I've done the same with sponsees. I have had a Spiritual Awakening as the result of these steps, and tried to carry the message to others. The biggest gift of my Spiritual Awakening is that my experience can benefit others! I just may

save another person's life by sharing my past.
This is only by the Grace of God, in my
opinion. God saved me from myself, dragged me
to AA, and taught me to love myself, love
others and be of service to others. That is
very different behavior from the days before.
My fondest reward of doing 12 step work is when
I see the light go on in a newcomers eyes, that
"I Get IT" moment.

My God as I understand him has evolved in
full circle, but settled on a mirror image of
my childhood God. Today, it is my choice to
believe He is unconditional love. No backhands
across the face, but warm palms holding me when
I need it most. His Son gives me examples and
lessons to strive for answers. The Holy
Spirit, to me, is an 8 foot tall sheriff, with
a gun of Mercy on one hip and a gun of Grace on
the other. I choose the sheriff image because
he has his eyes on me always, and I'll
surrender to him in a heartbeat.

I've spent time in the program of AA, and
I've spent time away from the program of AA. I
am here to tell you that, if you have
alcoholism like I do, the time away from the
program isn't pretty at all. I abandoned my

faith, I forgot all God had done for me, and I drove myself crazy, to the jumping off point. The loneliness I felt is beyond words. Yet, God saved me again, and gave me another chance proving to me that I am worth his attention, Grace and Mercy. I will not test his patience again. I have proven to myself that I have alcoholism that I wake up with it every day. I have a daily reprieve based on the maintenance of my spiritual condition. For me, it truly is One Day at a Time. I have been reunited with God, AA and a wonderful fellowship for just over a year again, and the rapidity of healing has been miraculous. I have been graced with a measure of love not known to me before. I give love and receive love in doses that would have crushed me not long ago. By the Grace and Mercy of God, it no longer feels strange to me to live in His light.

I have realized once again that the twelve steps work on every single defect of character in my life. One example... I admit I am powerless over sheet cake - my blood sugars have become unmanageable. I can practice gluttony if I don't pray for strength when I see cake. Step One is the most powerful step. The secret of step one is, in my opinion, that we work the step for some time drinking and using. If we survive ourselves and make it to a 12 step program, all we have to do then is admit it to someone. You are then on your way, through the 12 steps, to a new freedom and a new happiness.

The Fellowship in the 12 step rooms is unlike any other. We all come from every corner of society's map, every level, every background. Yet, we all have the common bond, and we cry and laugh at the same issues together.

Before, I would NOT mix with these folks, now I can't wait to HUG them. I have about 5 great friends, about 25 good friends, and about 100 folks I really like! The best evidence that a 12 step program works, these folks love me for who I am, and I no longer seek to drive them away. The 12 promises come true in my life on a daily basis, if I let God run my life. The instant I grab the steering wheel back, no telling where I'm going to end up... but most likely on my hands and knees vomiting again.

I used to loathe myself. Today, having had a Spiritual Awakening as the result of the

12 steps, I realize I am Graced by God to GET TO BE ME. I am the only one in human history tasked with the job of being me, and with God's help, I can be the best me for Him I can be. Today, I believe God believes in me, pays attention to me, and gives me another chance each day I wake up and hit my knees asking for His guidance and strength.

Thank you God for letting me be of service.

Veronica

"The bad times are only temporary…

and so are the good"

"Don't get old", they said, "if you're a real alcoholic there's a point where it stops working." Those two statements that I heard when I was beginning this trek to freedom stood out for me.

When I was small I vividly remember having thoughts of ending it all, not feeling loved, feeling abandonment, and feeling fear (but I'd never let you see that last one). I wanted the world to see the opposite that I was. Someone who was unbreakable and who could roll with the punches. My first reaction was usually anger. When I was a child and throughout my young adulthood, rage fueled me. It was a feeling so close to getting high and I was hooked, though I didn't know it yet.

I had everything I desired growing up and an unbelievable amount of love from my mother and Step-Father. My biological father was absent. My sister despised playing with me. Any

101

broken or misplaced part of shaping my young self overwhelmed me and lay heavy. I felt incredibly uncomfortable with others. When my mother sang to me, I wanted it to stop, when she reached for my hand, I felt pins run through my body making me uncomfortable. These are feelings that lingered and they intensified

Accepting love from anyone felt like internal torture.

Oh but that first drink, that first hit, I felt normal.

I found it, that thing that made me feel like my peers, at peace and comfort, and unbreakable in its truth.

I was 12 or 13 years old the first time I got blackout drunk, I would sneak drinks at weddings when I was smaller or take a beer here and there from the fridge but that was my first *"yes this is it"* moment. I wanted to feel free like I did when I was drunk constantly. I just didn't have the *"stop…ok you're drunk now"* identifier and I over shot the mark more times than I can count, blacking out 80% of the time.

I felt protected and safe in my private school and graduating middle school with 30 of my closest friends was spectacular. I was somebody, I had some friends, but I found my best friend. It was most importantly a friend that would show up for me in so many forms... alcohol.

High school was awful. I had never experienced public school before. I was climbing out of my skin, so on day two I filled a bottle with vodka and went to school drunk.

At age 15 I had my solution to feelings, good bad and the ugly, my liquid saving grace.

I also learned in high-school what I could use my body to get what I wanted. The older the man, the more he would supply. Most of my *friends* were in there 30's. I didn't think much of that until I sobered up.

I met **Him** in high school when I was 16. He was a vision, wrote poetry and smoked weed and drank.

Destruction began in full force, demolition of my dignity and self-worth when he left.

Again I felt abandoned by a man I loved. I started using meth and cocaine and I laid hands on my mother and moved out. I had seen what my peers had done to their families and I wasn't about to do the same. I moved in with my boyfriend in an R.V. in the backyard of a manufactured home. There, I could do whatever I wanted. I stayed in high school, no way would I drop out. I didn't want to be like the older men I lived and partied with, I had to graduate. I would show up to school in the same dirty clothing I had been wearing for weeks. I was physically, sexually, and emotionally abused by the men that I was living with in the R.V., so I started living in my car. I still kept a job, and remained in school. I had a sleeping bag and Styrofoam cooler set up in a shed in the Home Depot parking lot. I would collect it at 4 am before anyone would come and find them.

I was managing, I was in school, I told myself a lot of lies to keep moving what I thought was forward. Teachers and parents reached out to help me, but I was unbreakable, unbroken, invincible, and fearless don't you know?

I graduated and I was not going to go to college. I left for San Francisco where I knew it would be different, and it was. I found a victim of my love addiction with the inability to fully commit and ran shortly after.

But also in San Francisco I experienced young people living normal lives without rave

families and drug "habits". Something within me
and also "the man" encouraged me to go back to
Arizona to get a college education. We were to
get married in San Francisco and run away
together but he never showed.

I left for college leaving him too. Things
were going to be different, no "the man" or
drug connections. I was going to get myself a
college degree and make something of myself. I
would get that paper saying I was "worth
something"… solid proof because I didn't think
I was worth anything.

Again, that next morning I woke up in the
hospital, overdose and alcohol poisoning. I
didn't understand how? They offered me 9 days
of drug and alcohol treatment and I left before
they returned. I had to get that college degree
to prove I was smart... I didn't have 9 days.
Things were supposed to be different, I wanted
it so badly.

I white knuckled it throughout the day but
every night and even the morning I was smashed.
Something was wrong with my brain, I knew it
and I spent time researching brain transplants
and every other method to fix me, but I kept
drinking and using drugs. Shortly after, he

moved to my college town. He showed up one day with an R.V. and said "get in, let's get out of this bullshit and live our lives". I didn't go.

He was murdered two days before Christmas that same year. I tried to kill myself, I had gotten a few charges that sent me to alcohol and drug counseling and the courts required an AA meeting sheet for me to get signed. The night I took a handful of pills, I called a man in AA and he told me to go to the hospital, I made it to the lobby before I blacked out. Again I left before they sent me to the psych unit. I.V. in my arm and everything. I didn't have the time to sit I had to beat this.
I want more and need more, whatever is there I want to feel 0 or 1000 but not what I was feeling now.

I came back into the room broken, beat up and full of fear, but I kept myself within the walls of Fort Knox, I was not about to let anyone see that sad, disintegrating broken child. I got a sponsor and started the steps, but I was not willing to do the work, the real work, the looking inward and seeking Gods help. If God was real, he was a sick MFer to let the things that happened to me happen. No chance was I going to talk about the R.V. and the things I had to do to keep moving. No way! I had covered and re-covered; burnt and buried and drowned in drugs and alcohol to keep those things cemented 100 yards down.

I wasn't about to share anything about them. I wasn't able to piece together more than 28 days, I started using the one thing I told myself I would never use. It killed my cousin when I was small and I watched my family fall apart. That became my master and king alcohol became the sidekick.

I was in and out of the rooms for three years, wanting, needing sobriety but just out of reach of it. At one point I was at about 6 months sober and on my 4th step. That's where I discovered my personal struggle with not just stopping but staying stopped. Those things on my fourth step, well the things that belonged on there that I was not going to give up kept me sick. I worked so hard to pour drugs and alcohol on these things I was not going to dig them up. Those are the things that continued to take me out, guilt and shame. It was no longer about having fun. I was using to satisfy my obsession of the mind and the allergy of the

body. This disease feeds on the weakest bits of
my mind and thrives there. "You're a fuck up,"
" you're not enough," " why bother you're
already a piece of shit," ad infinitum. I
became beaten, battered into a numb state of
reasonableness. I was physically, emotionally
and spiritually bankrupt and broken. I felt
like and empty shell, the walking dead, a waste
of oxygen, I wanted to die. I hated myself for
being who I was. I wanted to feel the freedom I
saw sober AA-ers have.

I wanted to feel safe, protected,
confident, and courageous but I had to become
hopeless first. I spent that last night I used
curled into a ball, begging for freedom from
anything out there that heard me. I called both
my doctor and my sponsor and both told me they
could not help me. I needed something more.

No persons left to reach out to I went to a
power greater than myself. I knew that this had
worked for those before me, I saw "them" for
the past 3 years stay sober and gain soundness
of mind. I saw women carry themselves with
dignity and respect. I saw anger be lifted from
the souls of the heavy haters for humanity. I
knew it was real because of them. Those people
that showed up to carry the message not only by

their words but by the light that shown from their open eyes that were filled with life. I knew it was real, that miracles happened and I wanted mine. Fuck it, it was about damn time!

Like I mentioned I had to get there internally. My "bottom" was internal, I thought it was an external thing for so long, obviously it was not or I would have been there at bottom years before.

I set to work...vigorously. I spent some days, all day, sitting at the Alano club. {A place for AA meetings} When I had a feeling I did not recognize or a feeling that felt uncomfortable I went to the Alano club, I would go to meeting after meeting until sundown. I spent many hours on my sponsors couch or in the car or back of a motorcycle riding around, turning my head off and identifying that my feelings were not facts.

My skin had always felt so tight, when I got tight my skin felt loose and comfortable. When I got sober my skin was taken off, I was left with nerves and very little muscle for strength. Alcohol and his sidekick was my shield, my comfort, my best friend, and protected me from you and the world for so long.

When I got sober I felt everything, as if I had never felt anything ever before, and I turned to the fellowship and to the Big Book for strength. In the book of Alcoholics Anonymous I found all my answers.

Once I was at a conference and locked out of my hotel room, I was having a panic attack. I had become so accustomed to reading out of the book to calm down or do a spot check inventory but my book was left inside the locked room. I sat on the floor outside the room in tears and it came to me like a lightning bolt, I know the words in the book! I may not always have access to the book, but I always have access to that Power within me that I call God. I prayed and read from memory and realized then that if I kept close to God I had strength. The language was not important and neither was the tangible, what was important was that continuous growth in my relationship with God. That and only that would keep me grounded in times of fear.

At 27 years old and just over 5 years sober I have many experiences just like that.

If I am close to God I feel empowered and the opposite if I am not. Just after my 4 year birthday I changed jobs, well first I quit all jobs. I had 4. I still struggle with balance. 0 or 100% and no in between. I drove up the PCH in hopes of feeling freedom and life. I was done with my life as it was. I missed the years when I was 19 and hitchhiked across country looking for número uno! When I made it to Big Sur she beat me up real good emotionally and physically as I went during monsoon season. I am not a planner I am a runner and hope for the best.

I made it to Washington, and one day as the rain fell on the oceans beach I sat in my car and cried. I had cut my 7 yr. old dreadlocks off with kindergarten scissors and they sat there on my passenger seat. I hadn't showered in over a week. I had hidden behind them now for too long, they were not intended to be my identity. I had abused them the last year and it was time for me to remove the last bit of old life from my physical body. To be reborn and cleansed from "who you think you are."

I had another spiritual experience, I have a good life, a good family, good opportunity, and to throw it away like it's "not good enough" "I'm not good enough" is far too familiar to the voice of my disease.

I returned home with no hair and a hunger for success. I got my dream job a month after my return. I found a house and was approved for a loan on my own.

After the long process of investigating my income to close on my house I was fired. One week after signing closing papers I was jobless, my roommate left, I lost my health insurance, and I was abused by my partner, and was in physical pain beyond imagination. I fell apart. I went from bed to bath tub, tears pouring from my eyes, I could barely move. MRSA did me in good, I also have colitis and times of stress make this disease flare. Again I had lost all hope... This is my life at 4 years!?

God shows up in mysterious ways, my dad came over and carried me to the doctor. My sponsor encouraged me to not commit suicide and to get out of self. I prayed and went to a meeting. Chin-up, the bad times are only temporary, and so are the good. I made it to my 5 years and was angry, it was just another day, another week I worked 90 hrs., just to pay the

bills...no cake, no special party or rhinestone
chip, just another day sober.

Some days it feels like I'm just barely
making it through, and some days I'm floating
on the pinkest of clouds. But I know when I
keep close to God I can get through it all. I
also have learned that there is nothing that
God and a new comer woman cannot fix. I am
constantly learning. At times it is a painful
process. I know and have experienced staying
sober no matter what. I experience life so that
I can be of maximum service to those that want
to start this journey. I can walk hand and hand
with those affected as I was.

When anyone, anywhere reaches out for help
I want the hand of AA to always be there. I am
responsible. That is my purpose, my meaning of
life. I never thought I had one. I know today
my purpose is to be of maximum service to God
and to all of Gods children. God is willing;
the true question is....am I!?

JEFF

"My problem is Jeff"

On August 28th, 2010, I decided to go to a meeting of Alcoholics Anonymous. My brother had been 14 years sober at that time. I went mainly because "people" were worried about me and I was curious. I didn't think I had a problem with alcohol. I've always had a job, a place to live, never in and out of jail. I had never had to wake up and find a bottle.

I thought for sure if I told this to someone at this meeting they would tell me to go home and that I wasn't an alcoholic. Well…I was wrong.

My brother had told me to listen for the similarities, not the differences when people talked. He said if I could relate to anyone, that I should ask them to sponsor me.

I walked in the room before the meeting started. I looked up on the wall where the 12 steps were posted on a large framed picture and read the first four steps. I laughed to myself, this program is definitely not for me. I was

right back in grade school. I had seen
something similar to these steps as a child.

The meeting started. The chairperson asked
if there were any newcomers who were in their
first 24 hours. I stood up with some other new
people. I said my name and mumbled, "I am an
alcoholic". I picked up a 24 hour chip.

Some *crazy dude* from New York City spoke
for fifteen minutes. No similarities there.
Then some guy in the back of the room started
talking. He was sharing some things that he had
done and some things that had happened to him.
He was telling my story. I remember being
filled with fear and anger. I thought to
myself, *I am being set up.* My next thought was,
but no one knew I was coming to this meeting.

There was a sign on the podium which read,
YOU'RE NOT ALONE. More fear set in. Someone
said, "If you don't think you're an alcoholic
go out and try some controlled drinking." I
remember thinking - Yes, I can do that. (In
honesty, in 35 years of drinking and whatnot,
99.7% of the time I drank to pass out.)

They placed me at the beginners table. As
people shared I thought...*no similarity, no
similarity*...then it came around the table to

this Charles Manson looking biker dude. In a low raspy voice he said, "I am a drunk, and a dope addict and my problem is Will."

That's all that I can remember him saying. I remember thinking this guy seems cool. I had hung out with bikers and hippies back in the day. I'll ask him to sponsor me. *He'll tell me I'm not an alcoholic.*

After the meeting our group walked outside. I lit up a smoke. Will was standing there. I got very nervous. I asked him as I was shaking, "Would you sponsor me?" In a very loud and angry voice he said, "I don't know if I have time for you!" He continued, "I've had 20 sponsees, 17 are either dead or still out there. Only 3 have made it so far. Your odds are 1 in 50 and you probably ain't gonna make it, dude!" "Have you got a suit?" he continued.

I responded, "No." "Well," he said "You might want to get one because if you stick around here you will make some friends and some of them will die." "You'll be going to a lot of funerals," he continued.

I was ready to punch this guy. He was like 6'1" and I'm 5'6". I had that 1000 foot stare into his eyes….**I knew he was serious.**

116

You see growing up I was a bully and a fighter. (Not proud of that) I feared very few. I didn't take that swing.

He said, "Are you powerless over alcohol, and is your life unmanageable?"

"No', I replied, I could feel the blood rushing to my head.

"Can you come to believe that a power greater than yourself could restore you to sanity?" he said, apparently not caring what my first response had been. "What?!!!" I can feel the veins popping out of my neck. I thought this s.o.b. just called me insane. Mind you I have been called crazy pretty much my whole life but never insane.

He seemed unaware of my reaction to his insulting question as he went on, "Can you make a decision to turn your will and your life over to a "GOD" of your own understanding?"

At last a question I can answer.

"Yeah" I said "I guess." I had been brought up Catholic so somehow this question seemed more appropriate.

We walked back into the room and he gave me a Big Book (Alcoholics Anonymous).

117

He started to tell me his story. He had 18 years of sobriety at that time. He was a Vietnam vet, Army ranger, Ex-biker etc.

We talked for a bit and he told me, "come back tomorrow at noon and *don't drink tonight.*" I said, "OK. See you tomorrow."

I got back to my apartment and called my mom and dad.

For 14 years they kept asking my brother to take me to AA. He told them that he couldn't because I needed to want to go.

"Hi mom went to an A.A. meeting today." She started crying, "Let me get dad." Dad got on the phone and I told him what I had just told mom. "I'm proud of you Swede!" he said. Dad is of Swedish blood.

My mom did tell me later that he too had shed a tear or two after that phone call.

I was off to the bar to do some moderate drinking. I had like four beers in six hours. Yea! I told myself. I did it. I am not an alcoholic.

The next day I went to the meeting and met with my sponsor. I lied and told him I didn't drink anything last night.

When I go home I called mom and dad again to let them know I had made another meeting.

I talked with mom briefly and asked to talk to dad.

"Well…" she said, "He's not feeling well today."

My father had been in and out of hospitals for 40 years and lived in constant pain. He had rheumatoid arthritis and other physical ailments. What came over the phone was a feeling of sadness. I said, "Mom I don't think he's going to make it."

She got upset so I apologized and hung up. I got on my knees and prayed to God, "Please God, take him. Hasn't he been through enough pain?"

I was so angry. If there was a God how could He let this happen? Not just to my dad, but others as well. He died that night.

A couple of days later I flew home to Rockford, Illinois for my dad's funeral. I told myself I was going to be strong and not drink

119

or use any drugs. My brother was with me and Will, my sponsor, had given me his number.

At the reception I was "white knuckling" it. I was talking to my mom and some of my cousins. Mom had set a glass of wine down on the table behind her. As she was talking, something in my brain shut down. I remember I took a step toward her. I started to reach for the glass.

She said, "Jeffrey, are you okay?"

I snapped out of whatever trance I was in and said, "Yes mom, just going to start cleaning up."

As I walked away I remember thinking did *that just happen?* Fear set in. I thought maybe that's what these AA's mean about powerlessness.

I went out that night *to "Little Italy"* with some family and friends. It was tough but I didn't drink. I walked away from three potential fights. I did call my sponsor that night. Thank God he answered.

When I got back home to Arizona I went through the steps with Will. We started reading the book called the 12 and 12. It has the twelve steps and twelve traditions in essay form. A book Bill Wilson wrote after a few years of sobriety. It is a companion to the book Alcoholics Anonymous.

Will had me do a written first step.

He said "What I want you to do is to go way back and write down the truth. Have a big eraser because you're going to need it. The truth about you and what happened. List the people who you hurt and the people who hurt you. The drugs you took and how they made you feel."

I didn't want to go there and it wasn't easy. I did need that eraser. I did get through it the best I could at that time and shared it with Will.

After a year and a half into my sobriety Will called me out on what I had shared with him so long ago. He made me see I was going to my grave with some things I did and things I thought of as a child. He helped me to understand that as they say, *I am as sick as my secrets*. He helped me to be as peace with my whole story. I realized I was no different or unique. I was free.

I can't tell you how blessed I am. AA has given me my family back. A woman I love. A God I don't fear. True friends and a whole new outlook on life. A design for living that works in good times and bad.

Now all I have to do is practice one day at a time what I have been taught. To help others is the reason I am on earth. If I stop doing what I am doing I will lost everything.

Pray, turn over my will, go to meetings and help others. Sounds easy huh? Not so much.

My sponsor also told me, "You got a bad brain. Remember the second step?"

He's right. My thinking is my problem. My problem is Jeff. I think I will keep coming back.

God Bless

TONI

"Tender Mercies and Amazing Grace"

I begin my story with a title that reveals its ending. And it is this extraordinary ending that makes the story worth telling, and I hope, worth reading. It is a journey from darkness to light.

My name is Toni and I am a grateful alcoholic. I say these exact words most every day at a meeting of Alcoholics Anonymous. It is a room filled with men and women who a share a bond that occurs only with a shared experience of life and death. Like the survivors of the Titanic. All saved from near death to live abundant lives.

We share the spiritual recovery of the nightmare existence that only other alcoholics can truly understand. We want to help others to arrive at the "spiritual awakening" our program promises – and delivers. I have experienced the promises personally and they have been the most powerful blessing in my life.

We use the word "recovered" wisely, we have been taught life is a one day even one hour, one moment experience. We learn to live in the "now". It is the only moment one can connect with God.

It is only in the sacred now that we can receive the God-given clarity and strength, and choose not to drink. This existence, has revealed to me, how to manage all the other demons that create human suffering. Fear, doubt, greed, pride, confusion – all ego based qualities. We say ego truly is "Edging God Out" and it does.

It has been the amazing program of AA that has shown me the *way*. Trusting the process, asking for help, helping others all allow the hours, days, months well lived to turn into years. I am now in year 21 of absolute growth. Personal growth. This creates the life of the promises. Peace, Happiness, Purpose, Freedom and no regrets. And this creates my gift of a "happy ending'. And this quantum change is even more impacting as my "beginnings" were very, very painful.

Born into a family of alcoholics, my earliest memories were of drunken parties. My mother and her five sister; uncles and aunts, falling down drunk, screaming and fighting was a nightmare for a little girl. I have physical scars that came from broken glass and bottles. Once I was rushed to the hospital with a cut wrist.

This kind of extreme childhood insanity can result in one of two ways of "being", you become a fighter and a rebel or – like me, you go numb and become compliant, and a people pleaser. My "job" as a people pleaser was to do what others wanted me to do. Controlling people are very much attracted to people pleasers. People pleasers do not live their own lives, they serve others.

I grew up doing what I was told to do. Fear was my constant companion. So, of course, I excelled in school, got good grades and tried out for many different activities. I became a cheerleader, choir member, debate team, etc. By the time I was old enough for college; my mother was in her third marriage. Because husband number three was an educated man, college was to be my next chapter.

Accepted by the university considered the "best", I found my still scared, try harder, numb 18 year old persona going where others told me to go. Looking back on that time, I realize I was not occupying my own body. I lived in my head, which gave me the "orders" to do what I was told to do. For me, this was *survival*. Robotically, I tried out for plays when my professor said I should. My grades were good. I did not dare to get involved with any male. That too felt too dangerous.

All and everything changed at nearly 20 years old when I went to a fraternity party. Someone made me a drink. I drank and like "Jekyll and Hyde", Toni morphed into an entirely different person. The blackout came quickly. My biology was so loaded for alcoholism that I was actually an alcoholic that night. (There are others like me who are alcoholics from the first drink). And I stayed one for the next thirty years. I could not safely take one drink.

The next morning, like thousands of mornings to come, I promised myself I would be more careful...I would only drink two glasses of wine... I would count my drinks...I would wait an hour between drinks.

I know today the answer is never. Not ever have even one. That is the very definition of the disease. One is too many and a thousand are not enough.

I was a periodic, never a daily drinker. Because of that, I lived between the blackout times, a normal life, even a very big life. I graduated college, went to graduate school. I married a man who became Vice President of a large corporation. We had two children, lived in beautiful houses. We moved often. I had careers of teaching, was the Executive Director of large non-profits, and started my own company designing kitchens and baths. Sounds good? It was in many ways. I loved my family and tried so hard. But the periodic drinking created chaos. It kept me weak and mostly lost.

It was finally in this lost-ness of myself that I knew I needed to divorce my controlling husband, and find a way to true happiness.

My children were grown. I had become a therapist, very much wanting to help other women. I chose to move to Arizona. I believe that after all my confusion, I was right to go it alone. Two years after this move and after my last black-out episode I decided to go to an AA meeting.

The last episode involved the usual really scary things, a DUI, and embarrassing encounter with the police, humiliation and depression.

The desert helped, the independence helped me gain clarity. But it was in the rooms of AA that I found my "way". I felt it in my bones. I sensed it in my intellect - this was my new path. And yes, one moment, one day at a time my spirit woke up. I came alive. I found my people, my way, my God.

AA is inspired by God. I believe this. I live this.

DONNA

*"There was a chair waiting for me. All I had
to do was walk through the door"*

I believe I was born with the disease of addiction. There are many traits that all addicts have in common. Looking back on my life, I had those characteristics before I ever picked up a drink or a drug. I never felt that I belonged or that I was good enough. I always felt alone in a room full of people.

I couldn't find a reason or event that made me an alcoholic, addict and I tried for many years hoping that if I found the reason, I would be able to drink without problems.

I had loving parents, supportive siblings and all my needs were met. I had four brothers and a sister, all much older. I was 10 years behind my last sibling. I looked at my brothers and sister as parents because of our age differences. I was an aunt by the time I was three and I was always placed at the kids table at family functions.

My parents only drank at appropriate times and never drank too much. I knew that one of my brothers had stopped drinking, but alcoholism was never discussed.

As a child I remember that my mind raced constantly. I never felt relaxed. I remember asking my mother, "when is the girl in my head going to shut up." Her loud voice made it hard to fall to sleep. She explained that the voice in my head was my brain. I always wondered if those without the disease were able to shut down and relax. My head was like a hamster on a wheel, in constant motion.

The day came that the noise stopped. That was when I had my first drink at age 12. I felt at peace for the first time. Alcohol perfectly filled the hole in my soul.

I tried to fit in at school. I was a nice Catholic school girl, a cheerleader and I was popular. What didn't change was my feeling that I didn't fit in. To add to that feeling, I got pregnant at sixteen. I had been dating this boy for two years. He had a bad boy image with a leather jacket and motorcycle. My parents were devastated but they supported me in my decision to keep the baby. Somehow, I was not ashamed but I was proud and walked through the halls until my ninth month of pregnancy, which further confirmed how different I was from the other girls. At that time, people were not educated on the effect of alcohol on a fetus and I drank through my entire pregnancy. I was fortunate to have a healthy baby girl. I finished school and started college with a baby in tow.

When my daughter turned three, I moved across the country to be near my sister. I worked full time, went on with studies while I continued to drink and do drugs. When my daughter's bedtime came, I partied at home. My sister babysat on weekends, which allowed me the freedom to continue my partying ways.

Working full time, going to school, being a single mother and partying in my spare time wore me out. Just when I thought it was too much to handle, I was introduced to cocaine. When high, I could take on the world with very few hours of sleep. I thought I was having the time of my life. It never dawned on me that my lifestyle could be a problem. Early on, there was no consequence for my using. I married, had a son and became the Vice President of a large baking firm. I began to travel more and had a large expense account, which allowed me to drink and use more, as I climbed the ladder of success. When I was home, I was a soccer mom. Entertaining was part of my job and I always got excellent reviews. I always had my fifth in my suitcase for those lonely nights in the hotel room.

Eventually my work began to suffer and my marriage ended. The last episode with that employer was getting so drunk on an airplane that I failed to show up for an important meeting. I left them no choice but to let me go. That was my first wakeup call that drugs and alcohol were a problem for me. It was the first of many more downward experiences.

I found myself at the jumping off point. I entered my first residential rehab. It was the first time I thought of myself as an addict. I concluded that I was just weak. At an outside meeting, there was a birthday meeting for a woman in her early 40's celebrating 20 years continuous sobriety.

My first thought was what could have possibly happened to that poor woman so early in her life that she was forced to quit drinking. She explained she could do anything in life except drink. She also knew if she did what the program suggested she would never have to drink again.

I thought that I too would never have to drink again. If she could do it, so could I. I dove into the program with the same enthusiasm that I had used my whole life. I was told to find a God of my own understanding and I found loving kind God that forgave my whole life, up to that point. I did the steps, stayed in the middle of the fellowship and the promises were coming true. I was never happier. I heard others talk about relapse and I was determined that it would never be a part of my story. Unfortunately it became a big part of my story also. *A daily reprieve, it turns out, is only good for a day at a time.*

Life got busy and I got complacent. I took credit for my new success, thinking I had stayed sober on my own willpower, thank you. In sobriety the voices that haunted my youth were back telling me how wonderful I was and how I had accomplished so much on my own. I drank again.

My life was a rollercoaster for many years. The program, using and drinking, back to rehab until things got good and then back to drinking. The consequences always got worse the next time and the next time. My actions when drinking severed all of my relationships with all who loved me. It was too hard to watch me throw my life away.

While drunk, a near fatal car accident left me in a coma for several days. There was no brain activity and I wasn't expected to live. God blessed me with another chance and I repaid Him by picking up a drink as soon as I got out of the hospital. I was certain that I would be the one who would experience death before I could recover again.

The day came when the gift of desperation filled my heart. I knew the solution was there all along. I just had to walk through the doors of AA and find the chair that was there waiting for me. My ego and pride kept me out many times when I needed it most. I couldn't let it happen again. I had to get the solution from my head to my heart. I had to get honest with myself.

Life happens but today I have tools that get me through when the going gets tough. I thank God for the program of AA and I thank the program of AA for my God.

Epilogue

With the rise of deaths from opioids, pills, drugs and alcohol perhaps it is time to once again visit one solution to the problem of addiction.

Alcohol and drug treatment has escalated into costing hundreds of thousands of dollars. Many times the person leaving treatment program is leaving with more pills to rely on and is also doomed to a life of a solution of pills for an addiction to pills, drugs etc. Sounds like Alice in Wonderland. It is all backwards.

The purpose of this book is to shed some light on a solution that has been around for over 70 years. It has changed the lives of countless millions. The cost is free.

Hopefully the reader can identify with one or more of the stories and see that 12 step programs are alive, well and are still changing lives.

This is a journey through the looking glass. That looking glass is your mirror.

ACKNOWLEDGEMENTS

Lori – Without your belief and trust in what I write, my words become a dusty notebook no one reads. Thank you for everything.

Bob – My love, my husband, my first editor and my encouragement that I have something of value to say.

Karen, Olga, Silvana and Dawn – May our children no longer be lost but beacons of hope to others.

Kenny, Toni, Mena, Donna, Jamie, Jeff, Alicia, Steven, Courtney and Veronica – Thank you for sharing the depths and heights of your lives with such honesty in order to help others.

Dad – I am in gratitude for your life and seeing how a 12 step program can impact your life and bless all those who were fortunate enough to meet you in sobriety.

My children, my grandchildren and my great-grandchildren – May each of you come to know your heritage of sobriety and freedom, faith and hope and the knowledge that no matter the problem, there is a solution here and now.

Reader – If you are lost, know that someone is reaching out a hand to find you and call you friend.

Made in the USA
Middletown, DE
01 November 2020